italian
grammar
made
easy

Hodder Arnold

DER HEADLINE GROUP

Orders: please contact Bookpoint Ltd, 130 Milton Park, Abingdon, Oxon
OX14 4SB. Telephone: (+44) 01235 827720. Fax (+44) 01235 400454.
Lines are open from 9.00am to 6.00pm, Monday to Saturday, with a 24-hour
message answering service. You can also order through our website
www.hoddereducation.co.uk.

If you have any comments to make about this, or any of our other titles, please
send them to educationenquiries@hodder.co.uk

British Library Cataloguing in Publication Data
A catalogue record for this title is available from the British Library

ISBN-10: 0 340 904 976
ISBN-13: 978 0 340 904 978

First Edition Published 2005
Impression number   10 9 8 7 6 5 4 3 2 1
Year   2009 2008 2007 2006 2005

All illustrations drawn by Chris Blythe/Daedalus Studio
Typeset in 10.5/12pt New Baskerville by Servis Filmsetting Ltd, Manchester
Printed and bound in Malta for Hodder Arnold, an imprint of Hodder Education, a
member of the Hodder Headline Group, 338 Euston Road, London NW1 3BH.

CONTENTS

2 Nouns and Determiners

INTRODUCTION

Italian Grammar Made Easy is an Italian grammar workbook aimed at adult non-linguists, that is adults with some rudimentary knowledge of Italian, who do not necessarily know anything about grammar, but need to learn about it so they can progress beyond phrasebook Italian.

In the past, grammar has been seen as a barrier to language learning. It has put more people off learning a language than it has helped. Because of the way grammar has been portrayed, students were often made to feel that only those who could master 'conjugations' and 'declensions' could learn a language. In fact, you can drive a car without mastering the principles of the internal combustion engine – but if you do learn where to put the oil and how to check the tyres and fill up the windscreen wash, it does help!

Grammar is about recognising word patterns which give you a framework to a language; if you know the framework, you can 'build' new language of your own instead of having to learn everything by heart.

For those who already know some Italian grammar, short cuts are marked with ▶▶ to enable you to go straight to the information you need. If you feel you would like to have more in-depth knowledge about a particular grammar point, please refer to *Azione Grammatica* D. Aust with M. Zollo, 1997/2000, 2nd edition.

An interactive CD-ROM accompanies this book for use with a PC. The CD-ROM contains exercises from the book. Most exercises are recorded so that you can listen to a native speaker saying the sentences and there is a 'click on' facility to allow you to read the English translation. There is also some additional listening material which provides a useful resource and brings the language to life.

A simple guide to the parts of speech

▶ ▶ **If you know what verbs, nouns, pronouns, adverbs, etc. are, go on to 1.1.**

The most useful categories of words to recognise are:

1 Verbs – 'doing' words

Verbs tell you what someone or something is doing.

> I *am going* to Italy. My friend *booked* the flight. I *am going* to a meeting.

You also use them to ask questions ...

> *Have* you *seen* the film? *Are* you all right?

... and to give instructions.

> *Fetch* it! *Slow* down! *Help* me! *Wait!*

Verbs usually present the most problems, so the section dealing with them is the longest one and comes first in the book.

2 Nouns – 'naming' words

Nouns are the words which tell you:

- what something is:
  a *timetable*, a *train*, a *station*, a *town*, a *secret*
- who someone is:
  a *steward*, a *bank clerk*, a *baker*, a *student*

3 Pronouns

Pronouns are words which 'stand in' for a noun.

> Signor Bianchi is Italian. Signor Bianchi lives in Rome.

Instead of repeating Signor Bianchi, you can say *he*.

> Signor Bianchi is Italian. *He* lives in Rome.

In the same way, you can say *she* instead of repeating *Marisa* in the following sentence.

> Marietta works in Piombino. *She* works at the ferry port.

These are also pronouns: *I, you, it, one, we, they, me, us, them.*

4 Adjectives

Adjectives are 'describing' words. They are used to describe something or someone.

the *new* house, the *red* car, a *tiny* flat, a *wet* day, a *busy* secretary

5 Adverbs

Adverbs are words which usually describe a verb, e.g. they describe how something is done. They often answer the question *How?* and in English they often end in *-ly*.

He runs *fast*. She eats *slowly*. It comes *naturally*!

6 Prepositions

Prepositions are words which usually tell you where something is, e.g. *in, under, on*. Words such as *to, for, with*, and *without* are also prepositions.

1 VERBS

1.1 Talking about what you do

▶▶ **If you know what a verb is, go on to 1.1.1.**

You use a verb to talk about what someone or something does, is doing, has done, or intends to do or is being, has been or intends to be. A verb can be called a doing or being word.

 To find out if a word is a verb ask yourself if someone could *do it.*

I Which of these words are things you can *do*?

a walk   **f** computer
b trainers   **g** behind
c shout   **h** red
d invent   **i** listen
e loud   **j** before

Some words can be used as verbs *and* nouns or adjectives. e.g. 'Drink' can be a drink in a cup or part of the verb 'to drink'.

 Ask: Are they 'doing' it? If they are it is a verb.

II Which of the italicized words are being used as verbs?

a Jack and Jill are to appear in a *play* at the local theatre.
b They will *play* the leading parts.
c They *work* during the day in an office.
d After *work* they go to rehearsals.
e Tonight they are having a *meeting* to discuss the production.
f They are *meeting* in the theatre bar.
g They need to discuss *finance.*
h Local sponsors usually *finance* the productions.
i The producer *reports* that this time there will be no sponsorship.
j According to newspaper *reports* the sponsors have gone bankrupt.

1.1.1 About verbs: what is the infinitive?

▶▶ **If you know what the infinitive is, go on to 1.1.2.**

When you look up a verb in a dictionary, you will find the infinitive form of it listed first. This is the 'name' of the verb.

In English, the infinitive consists of 'to' + verb, e.g. 'to eat', 'to build', 'to paint'.

Here are some Italian infinitives. You probably know some of them already or can guess what they mean.

III See how many you can match up with their English counterparts:

a parlare		to wash
b preparare		to travel
c organizzare		to study
d entrare		to look at/check
e viaggiare		to invite
f portare		to prepare
g controllare		to speak
h invitare		to carry/take/wear
i lavare		to organise
j studiare		to enter

These are usually referred to as *-are verbs* because their infinitive form ends in *-are*.

Try to look for similarities between Italian and English. Some are obvious: for example *entrare* means to enter. Others are less obvious, such as *viaggiare* which means to travel (or to go on a voyage); another is *controllare* meaning to check, similar to the idea of 'control', which is of course another meaning for this verb. Don't be afraid to try out these little 'leaps of faith', thinking around the areas of possible meaning: your guesses will usually be correct.

The Italian infinitive is often used to give commands, especially on public notices, and especially when telling people not to do something:

Aprire con attenzione.   Open carefully
Vietato calpestare l'erba.   Don't walk on the grass!

IV Here are some more *-are* verbs. How many of them do you know already? They all have to do with food and eating. Try to pair them off correctly with their meanings in English.

a	cucinare	to sprinkle
b	cenare	to thaw
c	spruzzare ~ pisodama putsina	to eat
d	congelare ~ kailunutana	to mix
e	sgelare	to dine
f	brasare	to lunch
g	versare	to cut
h	tagliare ~ to ikotu ~	to freeze
i	mangiare	to cook
j	pranzare	to braise
k	mescolare	to pour

If you find it difficult to learn new words, try to find a 'hook' to hang them on: e.g. *cucinare* based on *cucina* – kitchen, which is like *cuisine* in French. Similarly, if you know *tagliatelle*, which means pasta cut into strips, you can easily remember that *tagliare* must be to cut.

More than 50% of English words derive from Latin, as do more than 90% of Italian words; indeed, one could say that Italian is modern Latin. Of course this means that if you don't know a verb, you can just say the English verb with an Italian accent: you have a 50% chance of being understood.

V What do you think the Italian for these verbs would be? Cover up the Italian and see if you can work it out, or join the correct pairs with a line.

a	to begin	terminare
b	to accept	valutare
c	to separate	pubblicare
d	to evaluate	navigare
e	to steal	girare
f	to sail	cominciare
g	to publish	separare
h	to turn	rubare
i	to continue	continuare
j	to end	accettare

Most verbs based on a noun or an adjective, and based on words 'imported' from other languages, are *-are* verbs:

pranzo	lunch	*pranzare*	to have lunch
film	film	*filmare*	to film
fax	fax	*faxare*	to fax
rischio	risk	*rischiare*	to risk

Group 1: *-are* verbs	Group 2: *-ere* verbs	Group 3: *-ire* verbs	
parlare mangiare	prendere scrivere	dormire servire	finire preferire

▶▶ **If you know how to find the 'stem' or 'root' of a verb, go on to 1.1.3.**

In English, we just have regular and irregular verbs. A verb like 'to dance' is regular: 'dance', 'dances', 'danced', 'danced', and a verb like 'to fly' is irregular: 'fly', 'flies', 'flew', 'flown'.

As you have probably already noticed, Italian verbs are more complicated. Italian schoolchildren have to spend years learning all about Italian verbs, but we can find some shortcuts. Italian also has regular and irregular verbs, but we usually divide Italian regular verbs into three main groups to make them easier to learn, depending on whether the infinitive ends in (1) *-are*, (2) *-ere* or (3) *-ire*; this last group has two sub-groups, as we shall see later.

The stem, or root, of the verb is that part which is left after you take off the ending. It is used in making the other parts of the verb which you use to talk about the past and the future.

VI Which group does each verb belong to and what is its stem? (Remember: take off the *-are*, *-ere* or *-ire* to find the stem.)

a	vendere	to sell	(2) vend
b	mostrare	to show	1 ____
c	cantare	to sing	1 ____
d	salire	to go up	3 ____
e	lavare	to wash	1 ____
f	concludere	to end	2 ____
g	ascoltare	to listen	1 ____
h	chiudere	to close	2 ____
i	lasciare	to leave	1 ____
j	prendere	to take	2 ____
k	scegliere	to choose	3 ____
l	portare	to carry, wear	1 ____
m	tornare	to return	1 ____
n	venire	to come	3 ____
o	dormire	to sleep	3 ____

Fortunately, the majority of Italian verbs belong to group 1 (-*are* verbs) and they are mostly regular. When we say they are regular, we mean they follow the same pattern, so if you learn one, you can work out the endings you need for all the others.

1.1.3   Irregular verbs

Some verbs are awkward and don't really fit into any pattern. They are called irregular verbs. This means that you have to learn them separately, and, of course, they are the verbs you are likely to want to use most. Fortunately, you probably know quite a lot of them already, although you might not be aware of it: for example, you probably know that 'I know' is (*io*) *so* or 'I don't know' is (*io*) *non so* but the infinitive is *sapere*.

Note that in Italian, the person word is only used when emphasis or clarity is needed, because the different verb person endings are clear and distinctive in both written and spoken forms.

These are the most important irregular verbs to learn, because they are the most used:

infinitive:	essere – to be	avere – to have	andare – to go
io form:	sono – I am	ho – I have	vado – I am going

Some verbs are only irregular in certain forms, and others are completely irregular. Many have predictable spelling changes only in some forms, often simply to preserve the sound of a consonant or to 'strengthen' the sound of a vowel.

Some verbs with irregularities in certain forms only:

porre	to put	pongo	I put
		pongono	they/you* put
rimanere	to remain	rimango	I remain
		rimangono	they/you remain
salire	to go up	salgo	I go up
		salgono	they/you go up
valere	to be worth	valgo	I am worth
		valgono	they/you are worth

* Note: this form of *you* is used for two or more people you do not know well (the formal plural form).

Some verbs with stem spelling changes (the forms given are examples only):

dovere	to have to	devo	I have to
		dobbiamo	we have to
sedersi	to sit	mi siedo	I sit
		ci sediamo	we sit
tenere	to hold	tengo	I hold
		tieni	you hold
uscire	to go out	esco	I go out
		usciamo	we go out
venire	to come	vengo	I come
		vieni	you come

Some verbs with special spelling changes (the forms given are examples only):

cercare	to look for, to try to	cerco	I look for
		cerchi	you try to
pagare	to pay	pago	I pay
		paghi	you pay

If you know the rules of spelling and pronouncing Italian, you might notice that in each of these verbs the -*h*- is being used to keep the sound of the *c/g*.

Note also that verbs based on an irregular verb follow the same irregular pattern, for example:

salire	to go up	risalire	to go up again
tenere	to hold	sostenere	to sustain
venire	to come	convenire	to agree
cercare	to look for	ricercare	to seek

VII Match the infinitives.

a to know how to   volere
b to see   andare
c to have   essere
d to go   sapere
e to be able to   dovere
f to have to   fare
g to want to   potere
h to take   avere
i to be   prendere
j to do   vedere

1.1.4 The 'persons' of the verb

 If you know about the 'persons' of the verb go to 1.1.5.

When we talk about ourselves, it is called the 'first person'. When we talk about or to 'you', it is called the 'second person'. When we talk about someone else it is called the 'third person'. Note that in Italian, the formal forms of you, *lei* and *loro*, use the third person verbs.

In English, we only change the ending when we are talking about he/she or it: 'I walk – he walks'.

	Singular	**Plural**
first person	I talk	we talk
second person	you talk	you talk
third person	he/she/it talks	they talk

In many languages the verb ending changes according to who is doing the action and you have to learn the pattern of the verb. In Italian, the ending changes in clear patterns to show who is doing the action.

 Fortunately, in Italian not only are the endings spelt differently, but they all sound different, so there is never any confusion about who is doing what: it is worth learning them thoroughly. This is also why the 'person words' are usually not needed.

	Singular	**Plural**
first person	(io) parlo	(noi) parliamo
second person	(tu) parli	(voi) parlate
third person	(lui/lei) parla	(loro) parlano

I	io
you	tu
you (formal)	Lei
he	lui (egli)
she	lei (ella)
we (my friend and I)	noi
you	voi
you (plural formal)	Loro
they	loro

Note 1. Notice how the formal 'you' in the singular and plural is written with a capital L; this helps distinguish them from 'she' and 'they' in written form.

Note 2. You may sometimes come across the alternative forms for 'he' and 'she' given in brackets.

Io, tu, lui, lei etc. are called pronouns because they 'stand in' for, or represent, a person or thing. Mr Smith – 'he'; Mr and Mrs Smith – 'they'; Jim Smith and I – 'we', etc.

Tu is only used when talking to a child, a relation or very good friend. It implies a certain degree of intimacy and should not be used to address an adult unless he or she invites you to use it; *Lei* is used for formal situations. The same is true in the plural with *voi* and *Loro*, though this latter form is hardly ever used now, and *voi* is used instead.

lui/lei, 'he/she'. No word is usually used for 'it' (but see 3.1.4), as everything in Italian is either masculine or feminine; even window and door are feminine words.

loro is used for any group of people (or things) whether male, female or mixed.

▶ ▶ **For more information on pronouns, go to chapter 3.**

VIII Which pronoun would you use?

a You are talking about yourself: I am speaking.	tu	io	lui
b You are talking about a girlfriend:	io	voi	lei
c You are talking about a male friend:	noi	lui	lei
d You are talking about yourself and a male friend:	lui	lei	noi
e You are talking to two little girls:	tu	noi	voi
f You are talking to a stranger:	Lei	voi	tu
g You are talking about a group of women:	lui	lei	loro
h You are talking about a mixed group or a group of men:	loro	lei	noi

IX Which pronoun would you use when you are talking about:

a your friend Paolo	noi	lui	lei
b your friend Maria	loro	lei	tu
c Signor Bianchi	voi	Lei	lui
d Signor e signora Larini	loro	lei	Loro
e Signora Bianchi e signora Larini:	loro	lei	noi
f yourself and your male friend	noi	voi	o
g yourself	tu	voi	io
h Paolo, Guglielmo e Maria	loro	voi	noi
i Signori Marino, Barilla e Ducati	noi	voi	loro
j yourself and your friends Silvia and Carla	loro	noi	voi

1.1.5 ▶**Fast track:** verbs

Verbs are doing words: You use them to say what you (or someone/something else) are doing and to ask someone what he/she is doing.

In English when we look up a verb in the dictionary it is preceded by the word 'to': 'to go', 'to drive', 'to eat' etc. This is called the infinitive.

In Italian the infinitive is identified by its last three letters, so it is the *end* of the verb which is important.

All Italian infinitives end in *-are, -ere* or *-ire*, except verbs like *trarre* and *porre*, their compounds and those of *durre*.

Each of these is a sort of 'last name' for a large family of verbs which share their behaviour and characteristics.

In English we just have two main sorts of verbs: regular and irregular.

In Italian there are three main groups or families of verbs:

-*are* verbs which are regular and -*are* verbs which are irregular
-*ere* verbs which are regular and -*ere* verbs which are irregular
-*ire* verbs which are regular (divided into two main groups) and -*ire* verbs which are irregular

In English regular and irregular verbs change the ending only when talking about he/she/it:

I speak, he speaks   I go, she goes   I fly, it flies

In Italian the verb ending changes for all the different people. The different persons are:

Singular	Plural
I io	we noi
you (familiar) tu	you (familiar) voi
you (formal) Lei	you (formal) Loro
he/she/it lui/lei	they loro

1.2 Talking about what you are doing now: the present tense

▶▶ **If you know about the present tense and when to use it go on to section 1.2.8.**

The present tense is used:

to say what you are doing now:	'I am reading'
to make a general statement about what happens:	'It rarely rains in southern Italy'
to say what usually happens:	'We go out on Friday evenings'
to talk about something which will happen soon:	'Mum arrives on the 7 o'clock train'

In English, we have two ways of talking about the present. We can either use 'am/is' or 'are' to say what we are doing now:

I *am* working.
My friends *are going out.*
It *is raining.*

... or we can say what usually/generally happens, using the verb without the *am, is* or *are*:

I *read* magazines.
They *are* vegetarian.
It *rains* every day.

In Italian, there are the same two ways of expressing the present tense, but the simple one-word form is usually enough to describe something going on at present unless you want a more vivid description, in which case the longer form is used. (See 1.2.1.)

Leggo il giornale.	I read/I am reading the newspaper.
Lavorano all'aeroporto.	They work/They are working at the airport.
Il signor Loreto prende l'autobus.	Signor Loreto is taking/takes the bus.

I   Identify the verb you are going to use when you say these in Italian:

a I am downloading my e-mails.
b My friend is ringing me when she gets home.
c She is accompanying her parents to the airport.

d We are going to the cinema later.
e She is fetching me.
f She is taking her parents' car.
g They are flying with Alitalia.
h They are visiting the museum.
i She is studying in Switzerland.
j After the cinema we are dining at the Ristorante Dino.

accompagnare, cenare, scaricare, studiare, andare, prendere, portare, telefonare, visitare, volare

1.2.1 Talking about what you are doing at this moment: the present continuous tense

▶▶ **If you know about the present continuous tense and when to use it go on to 1.2.8.**

As already mentioned, Italian has a direct equivalent of the English present with 'am/is/are', known as the present continuous tense. The appropriate part of the verb *stare* in the present tense is used with a part of the main verb which is equivalent to English '-ing' in this sense. This is called the gerund (sometimes the present participle). For *-are* verbs, this ends in *-ando,* and for *-ere* and *-ire* verbs, it ends in *-endo.*

II Here are examples for each person of the verb. Can you translate them?

a sto cantando
b stai mangiando
c sta bevendo
d stiamo lavorando
e state viaggiando
f stanno salendo

There are a few verbs with slightly irregular *-ing* forms which can be learnt easily.

REMEMBER: This form is not used as much as in English. The normal present is usually enough.

III Say what you are doing or somebody else is doing:

a I am working (lavorare)
b you are dreaming (tu – sognare)
c we are watching (guardare)
d you are reading (Lei – leggere)
e he is drinking (bere)
f they are eating (mangiare)
g you are travelling (voi – viaggiare)
h you are leaving (Loro – partire)

1.2.2 Talking about yourself: *io*

Remember in Italian the verb ending changes according to who is doing the action.

► ► **If you know about the *io* form go to 'checklist: *io* forms', p. 23.**

A *Io* and regular *-are* verbs

Verbs which end in *-are* in the infinitive are called *-are* verbs. The infinitive is the form you find in the dictionary when you look a verb up.

 A very large proportion of Italian verbs end in *-are* and are regular.

In the *io* form (or first person) of the present tense, all *-are* verbs end in *-o*. Try reading them aloud.

Infinitive	Meaning	First person	Meaning
arrivare	to arrive	arrivo	I arrive
ascoltare	to listen	ascolto	I listen
guardare	to look at/watch	guardo	I look at/watch
lavorare	to work	lavoro	I work
parlare	to speak	parlo	I speak
portare	to carry/wear	porto	I carry/wear
spiegare	to explain	spiego	I explain
studiare	to take	studio	I take
suonare	to play (music)	suono	I play
visitare	to visit	visito	I visit

Remember that all these Italian forms can also translate 'am ... ing', and that it is not necessary to translate 'am' going from English into Italian unless you use the present continuous for vivid descriptions (See 1.2.1).

 The *io* form of all *-are* verbs ends in *-o*.

IV How would you say these in Italian? Remember, *io* is only needed for clarity or emphasis.

a I speak English. Io _____ inglese.
b I study too much. _____ troppo.
c I am wearing jeans. _____ i jeans.
d I work in an office. _____ in un ufficio.
e I am listening to the news. _____ le notizie.
f I play the guitar. _____ la chitarra.
g I visit the town. _____ la città.

h I am watching the children.   _____ i bambini.

I I am arriving home.   _____ a casa.

j I am explaining the firm's   _____ la politica dell'azienda.
   policies.

Now cover up the right-hand side of the page and see if you can do them again. Say them aloud.

V   These are all *-are* verbs. Fill in the gaps.

    a _____ in un ufficio.   I work in an office. (lavorare)

    b _____ alle otto.   I arrive at 8 o'clock. (arrivare)

    c _____ la macchina.   I park my car. (parcheggiare)

    d _____ nell'edificio.   I enter the building. (entrare)

    e _____ il custode.   I greet the caretaker. (salutare)

    f _____ l'ascensore per salire   I use the lift to go to the sixth
    al sesto piano.   floor. (usare)

    g _____ le chiavi in tasca.   I look for my keys in my pocket.
        (cercare)

    h _____ in ufficio.   I go into my office. (entrare)

    i _____ i documenti nella   I look for the documents in my
    valigetta.   briefcase. (cercare)

    j _____ fino alle dodici.   I work until twelve. (lavorare)

> Choose five of the verbs which you didn't know before (or had forgotten) and which you think would be useful to learn. Write down the meaning and the first letter of the verb. See how many you can remember.

VI   How would you say ...?

    a I am going into this shop.   Io _____ in questo negozio.
        (entrare)

    b I am buying a new car.   _____ una macchina nuova.
        (comprare)

    c I am calling my secretary.   _____ la mia segretaria.
        (chiamare)

    d I'm trying this beer.   _____ questa birra. (provare)

    e I'm paying.   _____ io! (pagare)

    f I am sending a letter.   _____ una lettera. (mandare)

    g I hope it'll be hot.   _____ che faccia caldo. (sperare)

    h I am trying to answer the   _____ di rispondere alla
    question.   domanda. (cercare)

    I I am throwing out the   _____ via i giornali vecchi.
    old papers.   (buttare)

    j I love you!   Ti _____! (amare)

> Highlight any verbs which you think would be useful for you to use sometime.

Remember, the overwhelming majority of *-are* verbs are regular. The *io* forms of all *-are* verbs end in *-o*.

VII Complete these sentences with the right form of the verb in brackets and read them aloud.

a Io _____ inglese. (parlare)
b _____ in treno. (viaggiare)
c _____ una notte a Roma. (passare)
d _____ un taxi. (chiamare)
e _____ alla stazione. (arrivare)
f _____ nella biglietteria. (entrare)
g _____ un biglietto per il Pendolino. (comprare)
h _____ il treno. (aspettare)
i _____ nel vagone ristorante. (cenare)
j _____ un fax. (mandare)
k _____ un po' con il mio vicino. (chiacchierare)
l _____ il vicino a prendere un caffè. (invitare)
m _____ al mio migliore amico. (telefonare)
n _____ il paesaggio che passa alla velocità di 200 km/h. (guardare)

B *Io* and regular *-ere* verbs

▶▶ **If you already know about regular *-ere* verbs, go on to '*Io* and irregular verbs' on p. 21.**

Most verbs are *-are* verbs, so there aren't so many of these *-ere* verbs.

In the *io* form (or first person) of the present tense, all *-ere* verbs end in *-o*. Try reading them aloud.

Infinitive	Meaning	First person	Meaning
bere*	to drink	bevo	I drink
chiedere	to ask for	chiedo	I ask for
correre	to run	corro	I run
credere	to believe/think	credo	I believe/think
leggere	to read	leggo	I read
mettere	to put	metto	I put
prendere	to take	prendo	I take
rispondere	to reply	rispondo	I reply
vedere	to see	vedo	I see
vendere	to sell	vendo	I sell

* *Bere* is slightly irregular in that the infinitive simplifies the stem used for most forms: *bev-* ...

VIII   Which verb would you use?

a You have to <u>take</u> this medicine.
b He has to <u>ask</u> for his meal.
c She has to <u>run</u>.
d He has to <u>respond</u>.
e You have to <u>sell</u> your house.
f We have to <u>read</u> this book.
g You must <u>drink</u> Italian wine!
h You have to <u>see</u> what it is like!
i You have to <u>put</u> your name on the form.
j Don't <u>believe</u> that!

IX   Match the English and the Italian.

a I drink/am drinking ...   vendo
b I take/am taking ...   chiedo
c I run/am running ...   vedo
d I read/am reading ...   metto
e I sell/am selling ...   bevo
f I ask for/am asking for ...   corro
g I put/am putting ...   rispondo
h I believe/am believing ...   prendo
i I see/am seeing ...   leggo
j I reply/am replying ...   credo

 The *io* form of *-ere* verbs always ends in *-o*.

 Some have a special spelling or pronunciation change to 'reinforce' or preserve their sound (see p. 20, '*Io* and verbs which change their spelling in the *io* form'). The main ones are *conoscere*, *tenere* and *rimanere*.

C   *Io* and regular *-ire* verbs

 If you already know about regular *-ire* verbs, go on to '*Io* and irregular verbs' on p. 21.

 Most verbs are *-are* verbs, so there aren't many of these *-ire verbs*.

Like almost all verbs in the present tense, these end in *-o* when you are talking about yourself (in the first person singular). Practise saying them aloud, as it will help you to remember them.

	Infinitive	Meaning	First person	Meaning
'normal' -ire verbs	dormire	to sleep	dormo	I sleep
	offrire	to offer	offro	I offer
	partire	to leave	parto	I leave
	seguire	to follow	seguo	I follow
	sentire	to hear	sento	I hear
	servire	to serve	servo	I serve
-isc- verbs	capire	to understand	capisco	I understand
	finire	to finish	finisco	I finish
	preferire	to prefer	preferisco	I prefer
	spedire	to send	spedisco	I send

X How would you say the following?

a I am sleeping at my parents' home.   _____ dai miei genitori. (dormire)

b I am following you.   Ti _____ (seguire)

c I am leaving today.   _____ oggi. (partire)

d I hear the music.   _____ la musica. (sentire)

e I am offering a present to my friend.   _____ un regalo al mio amico. (offrire)

f I don't understand a thing!   Non ci _____ niente! (capire)

g I prefer e-mail to the telephone.   _____ la posta elettronica al telefono. (preferire)

h I am sending a message to my friend.   _____ un messaggio al mio amico. (spedire)

Now cover up the right-hand side of the page and see if you can still do them.

	Infinitive	Meaning	First person	Meaning
'normal' -ire verbs	aprire	to open	apro	I open
	coprire	to cover	copro	I cover
	scoprire	to discover	scopro	I discover
	soffrire	to suffer	soffro	I suffer
-isc- verbs	contribuire	to contribute	contribuisco	I contribute
	costruire	to construct	costruisco	I construct
	garantire	to guarantee	garantisco	I guarantee
	gradire	to accept (with thanks)	gradisco	I accept (with thanks)
	pulire	to clean	pulisco	I clean
	suggerire	to suggest	suggerisco	I suggest

XI How would you say the following?

a I open the door.	Io _____ la porta. (aprire)
b I suggest a visit to Naples.	_____ una visita a Napoli. (suggerire)
c I guarantee it will be good.	_____ che sarà buono. (garantire)
d I cover my car when it rains.	_____ la mia macchina quando piove. (coprire)
e I suffer every day.	_____ ogni giorno. (soffrire)
f I am building a house.	_____ una casa. (costruire)
g I am discovering the truth.	_____ la verità. (scoprire)
h I am contributing ten euros.	_____ dieci euro. (contribuire)
i I clean the house once per week.	_____ la casa una volta alla settimana. (pulire)

Now cover up the right-hand side of the page and see if you can still do them.

XII How would you say the following?

a I am discovering the news.	_____ le notizie. (scoprire)
b I am cleaning my car.	_____ la mia macchina. (pulire)
c I am opening a bank account.	_____ un conto in banca. (aprire)
d I am guaranteeing this cheque.	_____ quest'assegno. (garantire)
e I am covering the baby.	_____ il bambino. (coprire)
f I suggest we meet there.	_____ di trovarci lì. (suggerire)

> Say them aloud to get used to the sound of the words: which ones sound a little like the English?

D *Io* and verbs which change their spelling in the *io* form

Some verbs in each of the three verb families modify their spelling in the first person. This is to make the verb easier to pronounce or to give it a stronger sound. However, they all still end in -*o* as you would expect.

Here are the most useful examples:

rimanere – rimango	I remain
tenere – tengo	I hold
venire – vengo	I come
salire – salgo	I go up

Note also:

conoscere	conosco

in which the *io* form is pronounced with a hard -*c*-, though most of the other forms are pronounced with the 'sh' sound before -*e* and -*i*.

As always, compound verbs based on these behave in the same way, e.g.

ritenere – ritengo	I think/believe/consider
pervenire – pervengo	I reach/arrive at
risalire – risalgo	I go up again

XIII How would you say the following? Use the verbs in brackets.

a I am holding a pen in my hand. _____ una penna in mano. (tenere)

b I am going to go upstairs. _____ di sopra. (salire)

c I know Romeo and Giulietta! _____ Romeo e Giulietta! (conoscere)

d I have my hands in my pocket. _____ le mani in tasca. (tenere)

e I stay at home every Sunday. _____ a casa tutte le domeniche. (rimanere)

f I know that girl very well. _____ bene quella ragazza. (conoscere)

g I come home every day. _____ a casa ogni giorno. (venire)

h I am getting back into the car. _____ in macchina. (risalire)

i I believe she is a very intelligent woman. _____ che sia una donna molto intelligente. (ritenere)

Cover up the Italian. Can you still do them?

E *Io* and irregular verbs

Needless to say, Italian has a few irregular verbs which have to be learnt because they are used so much. Here are the most useful ones in the *io* form in the present tense.

andare – vado	I go
avere – ho	I have
dare – do	I give
dire – dico	I say
dovere – devo/debbo (both are used)	I have to/must
essere – sono	I am
fare – faccio	I do
morire – muoio	I die
potere – posso	I can/am able
sapere – so	I know/know how to
stare – sto	I stay, am (location, state)
uscire – esco	I go out
volere – voglio	I want

XIV Choose a verb from the list above and complete each sentence with the correct form.

a I want to play tennis with you. _____ giocare a tennis con te.

b I have an old racket. _____ una racchetta vecchia.

c I am giving you my good racket.

Ti _____ la mia racchetta buona.

d I have to book the court.

_____ prenotare il campo.

e I can bring some tennis balls.

_____ portare delle palle da tennis.

f I can (I know how to) play quite well.

_____ giocare abbastanza bene.

g I am not very fit!

Non _____ in buone condizioni fisiche!

h I am going home afterwards.

Dopo _____ a casa.

F *Io* and reflexive verbs

▶▶ **If you know about reflexive verbs, go on to p. 23, 'checklist: *io* forms' or p. 23, 'saying you like something'.**

We don't have an equivalent form in English but you probably already know the reflexive verb *chiamarsi*, 'to be called'. *Mi chiamo* means 'I am called' or literally 'I call myself'. Notice how the reflexive 'self' word is stuck onto the end of the infinitive. These are usually known as reflexive verbs because most involve the idea of doing something to yourself, but they are also sometimes known as pronominal verbs. When choosing a specific part of one of these verbs, start with the appropriate 'self' word: when you are talking about yourself, you use *mi* and the first person of the verb, just as normal. There are more reflexive verbs in Italian than in English, many of which are not expressed with 'self' in English. Notice how most of the following have the idea of doing something to yourself:

Infinitive	Meaning	First person	Meaning
addormentarsi	to fall asleep	mi addormento	I fall asleep
alzarsi	to get up	mi alzo	I get up
annoiarsi	to get bored	mi annoio	I get bored
arrabbiarsi	to get angry	mi arrabbio	I get angry
farsi la barba	to shave	mi faccio la barba	I shave
lavarsi	to wash (oneself)	mi lavo	I wash (myself)
pettinarsi	to comb one's hair	mi pettino	I comb my hair
riposarsi	to rest	mi riposo	I rest
sedersi	to sit down	mi siedo*	I sit down
svegliarsi	to wake up	mi sveglio	I wake up
vestirsi	to get dressed	mi vesto	I get dressed

* Note the spelling change in the stem of *sedersi*.

XV   How would you say the following?

a I wake up at seven o'clock.   _____ alle sette.

b I get up straight away.   _____ subito.

c First, I shave.   Per prima cosa, _____.

d Then I wash myself.   Poi _____.

e I comb my hair in front of the mirror.   _____ davanti allo specchio.

f I get dressed in my bedroom.   _____ in camera.

g I sit down in the lounge.   _____ in salotto.

h I get bored waiting for my friend.   _____ aspettando il mio amico.

i I get angry with my friend.   _____ con il mio amico.

j I fall asleep in my armchair.   _____ in poltrona.

Checklist: -io forms

When talking about yourself in the present tense, you use *io* (but only when necessary) and the right part of the verb.

To find the right part of the verb, you take off the *-are/-ere/-ire* ending.

You then add *-o.*

The most important irregular *io* forms to remember are:

andare – to go – vado
avere – to have – ho
essere – to be – sono
fare – to do – faccio

Check you know these other useful irregular verbs:

conoscere – to know – conosco – I know (a person or place)
sapere – to know – so – I know (a fact, how to do something)
dire – to say – dico – I say
venire – to come – vengo – I come/am coming

G   Saying you like something

Italian does not really have a verb for 'to like'. Instead, it uses 'to please' as a sort of 'back-to-front' way of conveying the idea of liking:

mi piace questa casa **literally means 'this house pleases me'.**

So, for a plural thing liked, the verb becomes the plural 'they' form:

mi piacciono queste case

Note that the verb agrees with the thing liked, which is the subject. The person liking is therefore expressed by a pronoun. There are other expressions which work like this; here are the most useful ones:

Verb	I ... (singular)	I ... (plural)	Meaning
piacere	mi piace	mi piacciono	I like ...
interessare	mi interessa	mi interessano	I am interested in ...
rimanere	mi rimane	mi rimangono	I have ... left
fare male	mi fa male il/la ...	mi fanno male i/le ...	my ... hurt(s)

XVI Say that:

a ... your head hurts   _____ la testa.
b ... you only have two aspirins left   _____ solo due aspirine.
c ... you only have one euro left   _____ solo un euro.
d ... you like soluble aspirin   _____ l'aspirina solubile.
e ... you find the film quite interesting   _____ abbastanza il film.
f ... you love soap operas   _____ molto le telenovele.
g ... you are interested in the   _____ i personaggi.
   characters
h ... your eyes hurt   _____ gli occhi.

1.2.3 Talking to someone younger or someone you know well: *tu*

This is the 'you' form, or the 'second person' of the verb.

There are actually four forms of 'you' in Italian: the familiar forms *tu* (singular) and *voi* (plural) and the formal forms *Lei* (singular) and *Loro* (plural).

You use the *tu* form if you are talking to someone you know well – a friend, a child or an animal. You do not use it to a stranger, a business acquaintance or an older person unless invited to do so.

There is a special expression which means to address someone as *tu* – *dare del tu*, more or less like 'being on first-name terms'. If someone says, *Possiamo darci del tu*, it means 'Let's use the *tu* form'.

 The *tu* form is easy, as in all verbs in the present tense, and in many other tenses, it ends in -*i*.

▶▶ **If you are not going to need the *tu* form, go to 1.2.4.**

A *Tu* and regular verbs

In -*are*, -*ere*, and -*ire* verbs, the *tu* form ends in -*i*; there are no exceptions. Remember that in Italian, all letters are pronounced except for *h* (never pronounced), so these endings are very clear and distinct, which is why the *tu* itself is not normally needed in front of the verb.

-are: (io) parlo – (tu) parli
-ere: (io) prendo – (tu) prendi
-ire, normal type: (io) parto – (tu) parti
-ire, -isc- type: (io) preferisco – (tu) preferisci*

* Note that with all these *-isc-* verbs, forms with *-isci* or *-isce* are pronounced with *-sh-*, whilst *-isco-* is pronounced with a hard *-c-*.

XVII What is the tu form of these verbs?

a buy		**f** sell	
b drink		**g** listen	
c live		**h** write	
d speak		**i** wash	
e watch		**j** work	

B *Tu* and verbs which change the spelling of their stem

A few verbs modify the spelling of their stem in the second person (*tu*) form to keep the consonant sound, or to strengthen the vowel sound. Verbs with a stem ending in *-c-* or *-g-* use an *-h-* to preserve the hard *-c-* or *-g-* sound. Some verbs with stems ending in *-i-* lose it before the *-i* of the *tu* form is added, and a few modify the vowel of the stem. These changes also occur in some other forms of the verbs affected. Here are some examples of each type, with the *io,* first person form given to show the change clearly.

Type of change	Infinitive	Meaning	First person	Second person	Meaning
Final consonant of stem	cercare	to look for	cerco	cerchi	you look for
	pagare	to pay	pago	paghi	you pay
Loss of final *-i* from stem	mangiare	to eat	mangio	mangi	you eat
	studiare	to study	studio	studi	you study
Vowel change e > ie	sedere (sedersi)	to sit	mi siedo	ti siedi	you sit
	tenere	to hold	tengo	tieni	you hold
	venire	to come	vengo	vieni	you come

XVIII Choose a verb from the list above and complete each question or sentence with the correct form. Then, if you are feeling adventurous, translate them into English.

a _____ a giocare a squash con me?
b Quale lingua _____ tu?
c _____ la carne?

d Che cosa _____ nei negozi?
e _____ tu o devo pagare io?
f Che cosa _____ in mano?
g _____ al bar con me?
h Ti _____ lì, o vicino alla finestra?

C *Tu* and irregular verbs

The Italian verbs which are irregular in the *io* form are also irregular in the *tu* form. Here are the most useful ones in the *tu* form in the present tense.

andare – vai	you go
avere – hai	you have
dare – dai	you give
dire – dici	you say
dovere – devi	you have to
essere – sei	you are
fare – fai	you do
morire – muori	you die
potere – puoi	you can/are able
sapere – sai	you know/know how to
stare – stai	you stay, are (location, state)
uscire – esci	you go out
volere – vuoi	you want

XIX Use the right form of the verbs in brackets to tell someone what they are like.

a You are too talkative. (Tu) _____ troppo loquace. (essere)

b You have got a spot on your nose. _____ un brufolo sul naso. (avere)

c You never go to the swimming pool. Non _____ mai in piscina. (andare)

d You always want to eat a pizza. _____ sempre mangiare la pizza. (volere)

e You can watch soaps every day. _____ vedere le telenovele ogni giorno. (potere)

f You are never at home. Non _____ mai a casa. (stare)

g You don't know how to speak English. Non _____ parlare inglese. (sapere)

h You go out wearing jeans. _____ vestito/a coi jeans. (uscire)

i You say you are good at sport. _____ che riesci bene nello sport. (dire)

j You have to be more honest. _____ essere più onesto/a. (dovere)

D *Tu* and reflexive verbs

These are formed in the same way as in the *io* form but the reflexive pronoun is *ti* instead of *mi*.

Infinitive	Meaning	First person	Meaning
addormentarsi	to fall asleep	ti addormenti	you fall asleep
alzarsi	to get up	ti alzi	you get up
annoiarsi	to get bored	ti annoi	you get bored
arrabbiarsi	to get angry	ti arrabbi	you get angry
chiamarsi	to be called	ti chiami	you are called
farsi la barba	to shave	ti fai la barba	you shave
lavarsi	to wash (oneself)	ti lavi	you wash (yourself)
pettinarsi	to comb one's hair	ti pettini	you comb your hair
riposarsi	to rest	ti riposi	you rest
sedersi	to sit down	ti siedi*	you sit down
svegliarsi	to wake up	ti svegli	you wake up
vestirsi	to get dressed	ti vesti	you get dressed

* Note the spelling change in the stem of *sedersi*.

XX Match the questions. How would you ask a child:

a his or her name?
b at what time he/she gets up?
c where does he/she usually sit?
d if he/she gets angry with his/her brother?
e if he/she gets bored at school?

i Ti annoi a scuola?
ii Come ti chiami?
iii Ti arrabbi con tuo fratello?
iv A che ora ti alzi?
v Dove ti siedi di solito?

E Asking a friend or relative if he/she likes something

As we have seen, Italian uses 'to please' as a 'back-to-front' way of conveying the idea of liking. To ask a friend or relative if he/she likes something, use:

ti piace questa casa? literally 'does this house please you?'

So, for a plural thing liked, the verb becomes the plural 'they' form:

ti piacciono queste case?

There are other expressions which work like this; here is a list of the most useful ones:

Verb	you (sg.)	you (pl.)	Meaning
piacere	ti piace	ti piacciono	you like ...
interessare	ti interessa	ti interessano	you are interested in ...
rimanere	ti rimane	ti rimangono	you have ... left
fare male	ti fa male il/la ...	ti fanno male i/le ...	your ... hurt(s)
andare di	ti va di ...		you feel like ...

XXI Ask if:

a ... your friend's feet ache   _____ i piedi?

b ... he/she has a plaster left   _____ un cerotto?

c ... he/she has any money left   _____ dei soldi?

d ... he/she likes running   _____ correre?

e ... he/she feels like going to   _____ di andare al cinema?
    the cinema

f ... he/she likes Roberto   _____ i film di Roberto Benigni?
    Benigni's films

g ... he/she is interested in   _____ gli attori?
    the actors

F   *Tu* and asking questions

To make a question in Italian, you can change the intonation by making the voice rise towards the end of the sentence, as in English:

Sei stanco/a?	You are tired?
Ti riposi?	You are having a rest?
Ti interessa il calcio?	You're interested in football?
Ti ricordi del giorno quando ...?	Remember the day when ...?

When extra emphasis or clarity is needed, you can also form a question by using the subject pronoun *tu*. In some cases you can place it at the end of the question. Of course this is not done often because *tu* is not usually needed.

Ma, abiti a Roma tu?	But, do *you* live/are *you* living in Rome?
Tu giochi a tennis, o a pallavolo?	Do *you* play tennis or volleyball?
Che preferisci tu, il teatro o il cinema?	What do *you* prefer theatre or cinema?
Hai ascoltato le notizie tu?	Have *you* heard the news?
Tu ci senti bene?	Can *you* hear well?
Tu mangi i frutti di mare?	Do *you* eat seafood?
Parli anche tu lo spagnolo?	Do *you* speak Spanish too?
Tu prendi l'autobus?	Are *you* catching the bus?

 Practise saying questions to get used to the sound. Remember to make your voice rise towards the end. You will probably feel silly at first, but don't worry, practice eventually makes perfect.

XXII Practise asking your friend what he/she is going to do. Just add the *tu* form of the verb in brackets.

a Have you got a meeting in   _____ una riunione a Roma
    Rome next Tuesday?   martedì prossimo? (avere)

b Are you leaving very early?   _____ molto presto? (partire)

c Are you taking the Pendolino? _____ il Pendolino? (prendere)
d Do you get in to Termini? _____ a Termini? (arrivare)
e Will you have dinner with us? _____ con noi? (cenare)
f Are you going back to Turin _____ a Torino la sera stessa?
the same evening? (tornare)

XXIII Chatting up – imagine you have already got to the *tu* stage
with somebody of the opposite sex. Match the phrases, then
cover the right-hand side of the page and see if you can
remember the Italian translations.

a Would you like a drink?	**i**	Vuoi una sigaretta?
b Do you prefer red or white wine?	**ii**	Sei stanco/a?
c Do you smoke?	**iii**	Vuoi qualcosa da bere?
d Do you mind if I smoke?	**iv**	Vuoi mangiare fuori?
e Do you want a cigarette?	**v**	Fumi?
f Are you hungry?	**vi**	Preferisci il vino rosso o il vino bianco?
g Would you like to go out to dinner?	**vii**	Ti dispiace se fumo?
h Are you tired?	**viii**	Hai il ragazzo/la ragazza?
i Do you like sci-fi films?	**ix**	Hai fame?
j Have you got a boy/girlfriend?	**x**	Ti piacciono i film di fantascienza?

Checklist: the *tu* form

You only use the *tu* form when speaking to children, pets
and people you know very well, or people who have invited
you to use it. You do not use it to older people you do not
know unless invited to do so.

The *tu* form sounds different from all others, so the actual
word *tu* is not normally needed.

The *tu* form of all verbs in the present tense ends in *-i*.
There are no exceptions.

Questions are formed by changing the intonation; for the
sake of clarity or emphasis, the appropriate pronoun is
sometimes used after the verb.

Negatives are formed by putting *non* in front of the verb.

1.2.4 Talking about someone or something else:
lui/lei/Lei

▶▶ **If you know how to use the *lui/lei* form go on to
checklist p. 35.**

This form is called the third person. In English it is the 'he,
she, it' form of the verb. An important thing to remember

is that this form is also used for *Lei*, the formal word for 'you'. As usual, the subject pronoun/person word is not normally used, because the verb endings are clear enough by themselves; however, *Lei* is often used, especially in questions.

 In Italian, there is no word for *it*. Everything is masculine or feminine. *Una casa* ('a house') is feminine, so you say '*she is old*'; *un libro* ('a book') is masculine, so you say '*he is new*'.

The third person form is easy to learn, as it has the same vowel as the infinitive form in the case of *-are* and *-ere* verbs, and ends in *-e* for *-ire* verbs. In other words, it ends in *-a* for *-are* verbs and *-e* for *-ere* and *-ire* verbs; there are no exceptions.

For almost all verbs the stem is the same as for the *tu* form.

tu parli	lui/lei parla
tu vendi	lui/lei vende
tu parti	lui/lei parte
tu finisci	lui/lei finisce
tu vai	lui/lei va
tu hai	lui/lei ha

The only exception to this is essere:

tu sei	lui/lei è

A   *Lui/lei/Lei* and regular verbs

The *lui/lei/Lei* form of *-are* verbs ends in *-a* (the vowel of the infinitive ending): (*lui/lei/Lei*) *parla; compra; lava.*

The *lui/lei/Lei* form of *-ere* verbs ends in *-e* (the vowel of the infinitive ending): (*lui/lei/Lei*) *corre; beve; vive.*

The *lui/lei/Lei* form of *-ire* verbs also ends in *-e* (like the *tu* form but with *-e* instead of *-i*): (*lui/lei/Lei*) *sale; parte; preferisce.*

Note that all of these forms are also used for *Lei*.

XXIV   Find the right part of the verb.

a Lei _____ molte lettere ai giornali. (scrivere)
b Zucchero _____ canzoni in italiano e in inglese. (cantare)
c Mio figlio _____ in Internet. (navigare)
d La sua ragazza _____ molti gialli. (leggere)
e Erminia _____ molti messaggi di posta elettronica. (ricevere)
f Il signor Melli _____ la sua casa. (vendere)
g La signora Peroni _____ comprare una casa. (desiderare)
h La banca _____ soldi ai suoi clienti. (prestare)

i L'avvocato _____ i documenti del contratto di acquisto. (preparare)

j La signora Peroni _____ il documento di acquisto davanti all'avvocato. (firmare)

B   *Lui/lei/Lei* and verbs which change the spelling of their stem

The verbs with modified stem vowel spellings in the second person singular (*tu*) form have the same changes in the third person singular *lui/lei/Lei* form.

Here are some examples, with the *io* and *tu* forms, to show the change clearly.

	Infinitive	Meaning	First person	Second person	Third person	Meaning
vowel change e > ie	sedersi	to sit	mi siedo	ti siedi	si siede	you/he/she/sit(s)
	tenere	to hold	tengo	tieni	tiene	you/he/she hold(s)
	venire	to come	vengo	vieni	viene	you/he/she come(s)

C   *Lui/lei/Lei* and irregular verbs

The Italian verbs which are irregular in the *io* and *tu* form are also irregular in the *lui/lei/Lei* form, the latter being the formal word for 'you'. Here are the most useful ones in the *lui/lei/Lei* form in the present tense.

andare – va   you go/he/she goes
avere – ha   you have/he/she has
dare – dà   you give/he/she gives
dire – dice   you say/he/she says
dovere – deve   you have to/he/she has to
essere – è   you are/he/she is
fare – fa   you do/he/she does
morire – muore   you die/he/she dies
potere – può   you can/are able/he/she can/is able
sapere – sa   you know/(how to)/he/she knows (how to)
stare – sta   you stay, are/he/she stays, is (location, state)
uscire – esce   you go out/he/she goes out
volere – vuole   you want/he/she wants

XXV   Choose a verb from the lists above and complete each sentence with the correct form. Then, if you are feeling adventurous, translate them into English.

a Francesca _____ al cinema ogni domenica.

b Suo fratello _____ che questo è troppo.

c Un giorno, lei non _____ andare perché non c'è spettacolo.

d Lui non _____ che fare, perché sua sorella si annoia facilmente.

e _____ andare alla spiaggia con sua sorella.

f Ma lei _____ stare con le sue amiche.

g Finalmente, lei _____ per andare al bar.

h Allora, il fratello _____ rimanere a casa.

i Si _____ in poltrona.

j Il povero ragazzo _____ di noia!

XXVI How would you say the following? You can assume that any verbs not listed as irregular will be regular.

a Il signor Piccini _____ milanese. (essere)

b _____ andare a Reggio Calabria. (volere)

c _____ prendere il treno. (dovere)

d _____ alla stazione. (andare)

e _____ che deve stare una notte in treno. (sapere)

f Il giorno dopo, _____ a Reggio. (arrivare)

g _____ due valigie. (avere)

h _____ le valigie su un carrello. (mettere)

i _____ un taxi. (chiamare)

j Quando _____ al carrello, e prende le valigie. (tornare)

D *Lui/lei/Lei* and reflexive verbs

The reflexive pronoun for the *lui/lei* and *Lei* forms is *si*. In the following table, all the third person forms are also used for *Lei*, the formal way of expressing 'you'.

In normal (i.e. non-reflexive) verbs this form is often used to describe an action for which there is no known or stated subject:

Questo vino si vende al litro.　　This wine is sold by the litre.

Infinitive	Meaning	Third person	Meaning
addormentarsi	to fall asleep	si addormenta	(s)he/you fall(s) asleep
alzarsi	to get up	si alza	(s)he/you get(s) up
annoiarsi	to get bored	si annoia	(s)he/you get(s) bored
arrabbiarsi	to get angry	si arrabbia	(s)he/you get(s) angry
chiamarsi	to be called	si chiama	(s)he is/you are called
farsi la barba	to shave	si fa la barba	he/you shave(s)
lavarsi	to wash (oneself)	si lava	(s)he/you wash(es) (... self)

Infinitive	Meaning	Third person	Meaning
pettinarsi	to comb one's hair	si pettina	(s)he/you comb(s) ... hair
riposarsi	to rest	si riposa	(s)he/you rest(s)
sedersi	to sit down	si siede	(s)he/you sit(s) down
svegliarsi	to wake up	si sveglia	(s)he/you wake(s) up
vestirsi	to get dressed	si veste	(s)he/you get(s) dressed

XXVII *Che fa Luigi?* Use the correct form of the verb given.

a _____ alle undici. (svegliarsi)
b _____ a mezzogiorno. (alzarsi)
c _____ (farsi la barba)
d _____ un poco. (lavarsi)
e _____ con l'asciugamano. (asciugarsi)
f _____ (pettinarsi)
g _____ (vestirsi)
h _____ i denti. (lavarsi)
i _____ a leggere il giornale. (sedersi)
j _____ presto. (annoiarsi)
k _____ a correre per il parco. (mettersi)
l Dopo un'ora _____ (stancarsi)
m _____ fino all'ora di cena. (riposarsi)

E *Lei*: the formal form of 'you'

XXVIII Ask a stranger these questions, selecting the right form of the appropriate verb to complete the question.

a Would you like to come into the restaurant? _____ entrare nel ristorante?
b Do you smoke? _____ Lei?
c Do you eat meat? _____ la carne?
d Do you drink wine? _____ il vino?
e Do you prefer red or white wine? _____ il vino rosso o il vino bianco?

F *Lei* and asking questions

When extra emphasis or clarity is needed, you can also make a question by using the subject pronoun *Lei*. In some cases you can place it at the end of the question. Of course this is not done often because *Lei* is not usually needed.

Lei è stanco/a? — You are tired?
Lei si riposa? — You are having a rest?
Le interessa il calcio? — You're interested in football?

Si ricorda quando ...?	Do you remember the day when ...?
Abita a Venezia Lei?	Do you live/Are you living in Venice?
Gioca a squash?	Do you play/Are you playing squash?

Practise saying questions to get used to the sound. Remember to make your voice rise towards the end. You will probably feel silly at first, but don't worry, practice eventually makes perfect.

XXIX Practise asking your new business acquaintance what he/she is going to do. Just add the *Lei* form of the verb in brackets.

a Have you got a meeting in Milan next Wednesday? _____ una riunione a Milano mercoledì prossimo? (avere)

b Are you leaving very early? _____ molto presto? (partire)

c Are you taking the Pendolino? _____ il Pendolino? (prendere)

d What time do you arrive? A che ora _____? (arrivare)

e Are you having dinner at the hotel? _____ albergo? (cenare)

f Are you going back to Rome on Thursday? _____ a Roma giovedì? (tornare)

G Asking whether somebody else likes something

As we have seen before, Italian uses 'to please' as a 'back-to-front' way of conveying the idea of liking. The thing that changes is the personal pronoun which goes in front of the verb *piacere*: *gli* for 'to him', *le* for 'to her', *Le* for 'to you' (the formal form).

gli/le piace questa casa? Does s/he like ...? literally 'Does this house please him/her'?

So, for a plural thing liked, the verb changes to *piacciono*:

gli/le piacciono queste case 'S/he likes these houses' literally 'These houses are pleasing to him/her'.

H To ask whether a stranger likes something:

| Le piace questa gonna? | Do you like this skirt? |
| Le piacciono questi guanti? | Do you like these gloves? |

Remember that the subject of the verb is the thing liked, and that the person liking is expressed by a pronoun; the same happens with other similar expressions; see section 1.9.6.

I Using the *Lei* form

XXX Your employee is slacking ... Tell him/her what he/she is doing

a You read the paper in the morning.
(Lei) _____ il giornale la mattina. (leggere)

b You go to the toilet 8 times a day.
_____ al bagno 8 volte al giorno. (andare)

c You take 2 hours for your lunch break.
_____ due ore per il pranzo. (prendere)

d You sleep the best part of the afternoon.
_____ per la maggior parte del pomeriggio. (dormire)

e You do the crossword in the afternoon.
_____ il cruciverba nel pomeriggio. (fare)

f You drink a Scotch at tea time.
_____ un whisky all'ora del tè. (prendere)

g You have to work more.
_____ lavorare di più. (dovere)

h What do you say in your defence?
Che _____ Lei in sua difesa? (dire)

Checklist: the *lui/lei/Lei* forms

You use the *lui/lei/Lei* verb form when you are talking about someone or something, or when addressing somebody by the formal 'you' form, *Lei*.

The *lui/lei/Lei* endings of *-are* and *-ere* verbs use the vowel of the infinitive ending.

The *lui/lei/Lei* form of regular *-are* verbs ends in *-a*.

The *lui/lei/Lei* form of regular *-ere* and *-ire* verbs is made by adding *-e* to the stem.

The most common irregular verbs are andare (*va*), avere (*ha*), essere (*è*) and fare (*fa*).

The reflexive pronoun for the *lui/lei/Lei* form is *si:* come *si chiama?*

1.2.5 Talking about yourself and someone else: *noi*

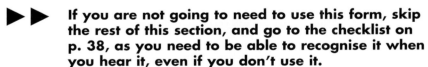

▶▶ **If you are not going to need to use this form, skip the rest of this section, and go to the checklist on p. 38, as you need to be able to recognise it when you hear it, even if you don't use it.**

You use the *noi* form (or the first person plural) where you use *we* in English, i.e. when talking about yourself and someone else: 'we', 'my husband and I', 'my colleagues and I', 'my friend and I', 'Mrs Brown and I', etc.

A   The *noi* form of regular verbs

The *noi* form is regular in almost all verbs. It is made by adding *-iamo* to the stem of *-are, -ere* and *-ire* verbs. Remember that in Italian, because the verb ending is very distinctive, the subject pronoun does not usually need to be expressed.

The *noi* form of irregular verbs tends to be close to the infinitive. This form is not affected by stem vowel changes, but does need the same spelling change with verbs whose stem ends in *-c-* and *-g-*, as we saw with the *tu* form of these verbs. This is to preserve the hard *-c-* or *-g-* before the *-i-* of the ending by adding an *-h-*. A couple of examples are included with the regular verbs below. Can you spot them?

Remember: the stem is made by taking the *-are/-ere/-ire* off the infinitive. See 1.1.2.

Note that this form is often used with the idea of 'Let's ...'

| Andiamo! | Let's go! |
| Mangiamo! | Let's eat! |

The table below shows some common regular verbs in the *noi* form; remember that each can be used for 'we ...' or 'we are ... ing':

Infinitive	Meaning	First person plural	Meaning
cambiare	to change	cambiamo	we change
capire	to understand	capiamo	we understand
finire*	to finish	finiamo	we finish
giocare	to play	giochiamo	we play
lavorare	to work	lavoriamo	we work
mangiare	to eat	mangiamo	we eat
pagare	to pay	paghiamo	we pay
parlare	to speak	parliamo	we speak
prendere	to take	prendiamo	we take
rimanere	to stay	rimaniamo	we stay
scegliere	to choose	scegliamo	we choose

*Notice that *-ire*: *-isc-* verbs do not have the *-isc-* in the *noi* form.

B   The *noi* form of irregular verbs

All verbs end in *-iamo*. The only verbs with an irregular *noi* form are:

Infinitive	Meaning	First person plural	Meaning
avere	to have	abbiamo	we have
dire	to say	diciamo	we say
dovere	to have to	dobbiamo	we have to
essere	to be	siamo	we are
fare	to do/make	facciamo	we do/make
potere	to be able	possiamo	we are able/can
sapere	to know	sappiamo	we know
uscire	to go out	usciamo	we go out
volere	to want	vogliamo	we want

XXXI How would you say the following? Use the verb given at the end of the sentence.

    a We are working today.   Oggi _____ . (lavorare)

    b We are playing volleyball tonight.   _____ a pallavolo questa sera. (giocare)

    c We are meeting friends at 6 p.m.   _____ degli amici alle 18. (vedere)

    d We are dining in a good restaurant.   _____ in un buon ristorante. (cenare)

    e We are going home at 10 p.m.   _____ a casa alle 22. (tornare)

    f We are going to Terracina tomorrow.   _____ a Terracina domani. (andare)

    g We are leaving at 8 a.m.   _____ alle 8. (partire)

    h We arrive at 11.15 a.m.   _____ alle 11.15. (arrivare)

    i We buy our tickets at the station.   _____ i biglietti alla stazione. (comprare)

    j We have lots of suitcases.   _____ molte valigie. (avere)

XXXII How would you say the following in Italian?

    a We are English.   Noi _____ inglesi.

    b We speak Italian.   _____ italiano.

    c We are going to Italy.   _____ in Italia.

    d We are choosing the departure day.   _____ il giorno della partenza.

    e We are taking the train.   _____ il treno.

    f We change trains in Milan.   _____ treno a Milano.

    g We understand the instructions.   _____ le istruzioni.

    h We stay in a hotel.   _____ in un albergo.

    i We eat in a restaurant.   _____ in un ristorante.

    j We are doing overtime work this evening.   _____ del lavoro straordinario questa sera.

    k We finish at 6 p.m.   _____ alle 18.

    l We are playing tennis later.   _____ a tennis più tardi.

C *Noi* with reflexive verbs

The reflexive form is made by adding *ci* in front of the verb, whether or not *noi* is expressed.

(Noi) ci chiamiamo Neil e John.　　　We are called Neil and John.

Infinitive	Meaning	First person plural	Meaning
addormentarsi	to fall asleep	ci addormentiamo	we fall asleep
alzarsi	to get up	ci alziamo	we get up
lavarsi	to wash	ci laviamo	we get washed
riposarsi	to rest	ci riposiamo	we rest
sedersi	to sit down	ci sediamo*	we sit down
separarsi	to get separated	ci separiamo	we get separated
svegliarsi	to wake up	ci svegliamo	we wake up
vestirsi	to get dressed	ci vestiamo	we get dressed

* Notice that there is no need for a vowel change in this form of *sedersi.*

XXXIII　　How would you say the following?

a We wake up at seven o'clock.　　_____ alle sette. (svegliarsi)
b We get up at eight o'clock.　　_____ alle otto. (alzarsi)
c We are getting washed.　　_____ (lavarsi)
d We are having a rest.　　_____ (riposarsi)
e We are getting dressed.　　_____ (vestirsi)
f We sit down on a sofa.　　_____ su un divano. (sedersi)
g We fall asleep.　　_____ (addormentarsi)
h We are getting separated.　　_____ (separarsi)

D Saying that you and others like something

As we have seen, Italian uses 'to please' as a 'back-to-front' way of conveying the idea of liking. To say that you and (an)other(s) like something, use *piace*:

ci piace questa spiaggia　　　　literally 'this beach pleases us'

So, for a plural thing liked, the verb becomes *piacciono*:

ci piacciono queste arance　　　we like these oranges

For similar 'back-to-front' expressions, see section 1.9.6.

Checklist: the *noi* form

To talk about yourself and someone else (*we*), use the *noi* form in Italian.

All verbs end in *-iamo.*

XXXIV   Match these English verbs with their Italian counterparts.

a	we have	vogliamo
b	we are	leggiamo
c	we are staying	veniamo
d	we are eating	non capiamo
e	we can	possiamo
f	we are not coming	siamo
g	we do not understand	arriviamo
h	we want	rimaniamo
i	we are going	abbiamo
j	we are seeing	facciamo
k	we are leaving	non veniamo
l	we are arriving	andiamo
m	we are coming	mangiamo
n	we are doing	partiamo
o	we are reading	vediamo

Now cover up the Italian and see if you can do them without help.

1.2.6   Talking to more than one person you know well: *voi*

▶▶   **Know about the *voi* form? Go to checklist p. 41**

This is the plural equivalent of the *tu* form, and so is used with more than one person, followed by its own form of the verb. Although it is 'familiar plural' form, it is very often used instead of the formal plural *Lei* form.

The *voi* form always ends in *-ate, -ete* or *-ite.*

A   *Voi* and regular verbs

The *voi* form is always made by adding *-ate, -ete* or *-ite* to the stem of the infinitive, and there are only two useful irregular verbs in this form, so it is very easy to learn. As usual, the subject pronoun is usually unnecessary because the endings are so distinctive.

Parlate inglese?	Do you speak English?
Avete una macchina italiana?	Have you got an Italian car?
Abitate in Italia?	Do you live in Italy?

The two most useful irregular *voi* forms are:

bere – bevete	you drink
essere – siete	you are

B   *Voi* and asking questions

▶▶   **Know all about asking questions? Go straight to 1.2.7.**

Questions are formed in the same way as in the *tu* and *Lei* forms: by changing the intonation. Occasionally, for emphasis, the pronoun is used, in which case it will usually come at the end of the question.

XXXV   Cover up the Italian and see if you can ask these questions.

a Are *you* going to the meeting?	Andate alla riunione voi?
b Have you got an appointment?	Avete un appuntamento?
c Do you know the MD?	Conoscete il direttore?
d Can you operate the video link-up?	Sapete usare l'apparecchio per la videoconferenza?
e Can you contact your boss?	Potete contattare il vostro capo?
f Do you have to go back to the hotel?	Dovete tornare in albergo?
g Do you want to use the OHP?	Volete usare la lavagna luminosa?
h Can you see the screen well?	Vedete bene lo schermo?
i Do you take notes?	Prendete appunti?
j Are you making recordings?	Fate delle registrazioni?
k Are you ready?	Siete pronti?
l Do you understand?	Capite bene?

C   *Voi* and reflexive verbs

The reflexive pronoun for the *voi* form is *vi* for both masculine and feminine.

Vi riposate il pomeriggio.	You have a rest in the afternoon.
Vi occupate del bambino.	You are looking after the child.
A che ora vi svegliate?	What time do you wake up?
A che ora vi alzate?	What time do you get up?

XXXVI   Match the following English and Italian phrases, then cover up the right-hand side and see if you can remember the Italian.

a Can you remember this man?	Vi vestite già?
b Are you having a rest?	Vi alzate tardi?
c Are you getting dressed already?	Vi svegliate presto?
d Are you having fun?	Vi ricordate di questo signore?
e Do you get up late ?	Vi riposate?
f Do you wake up early?	Vi divertite?

D   Asking others if they like something

As we have seen, Italian uses 'to please' as a 'back-to-front' way of conveying the idea of liking. To ask whether the people you are talking to like something, use *piace*:

vi piace questa piazza?	literally 'does this square please you?'

So, for a plural thing liked, the verb becomes piacciono:

vi piacciono queste mele?	do you like these apples?

For similar 'back-to-front' expressions, see 1.9.6.

Checklist: the *voi* form

The *voi* form is used when talking to two or more people or telling them what to do.

You are quite likely to use the *voi* form to ask polite questions to two or more people:

Potete dirmi come andare a ....?	Can you tell me the way to ... ?
Sapete ...?	Do you know (how to do something)?
Conoscete la signora Yannetta?	Do you know Mrs Yannetta?
Dove abitate?	Where do you live?

The *voi* form of regular verbs is made by adding *-ate/-ete/-ite* to the stem of the infinitive.

 Almost all verbs are regular.

Questions are formed by intonation:

Avete una macchina?	Have you got a car?

Reflexive verbs add the pronoun *vi*:

Vi alzate presto!	You get up early!

1.2.7 Talking about other people and things: *loro/Loro*

This form is called the third person plural. In English it is the 'they' form of the verb. In fact, *Loro*, the plural form of 'you', is not often used, the *voi* form being used for most cases of 'you' (pl.). As usual, the subject pronoun/person word is not normally used, because the verb endings are clear enough by themselves; however, *Loro* is sometimes used in questions.

▶▶ **If you know all about the *loro* form go to checklist p. 44.**

A *Loro* and regular *-are* verbs

The *loro* form is the same as the *lui/lei/Lei* form of the verb, but with *-no* added. As ever, the subject pronoun is usually unnecessary.

(lei) parla – she is talking   (loro) parlano – they are talking
(lui) studia – he is studying   (loro) studiano – they are studying

B *Loro* and regular *-ere/-ire* verbs

Again, the *loro/Loro* form has the same stem as the *lui/lei/Lei* form: replace the final *-e* with *-ono*.

(lui) prende – he takes, is taking (loro) prendono – they take, are taking

(lei) parte – she is leaving   (loro) partono – they are leaving

C *Loro* and irregular verbs

In fact, these are often similar to the *io* forms, owing to the effect of the *-o-* on the preceding consonant. The most useful irregular forms are in the following table.

Infinitive	Meaning	First person sing.	Third person pl.	Meaning
andare	to go	vado	vanno	they go
avere	to have	ho	hanno	they have
bere	to drink	bevo	bevono	they drink
dare	to give	do	danno	they give
dire	to say	dico	dicono	they say
dovere	to have to	devo/debbo	devo/debbo	they have to
essere	to be	sono*	sono*	they are
fare	to do/make	faccio	fanno	they do/make
potere	to be able	posso	possono	they can
rimanere	to stay	rimango	rimangono	they stay
salire	to go up	salgo	salgono	they go up
sapere	to know	so	sanno	they know
sedersi	to sit down	mi siedo	si siedono	they sit down
stare	to be, stay	sto	stanno	they are/stay
tenere	to hold	tengo	tengono	they hold
uscire	to go out	esco	escono	they go out
venire	to come	vengo	vengono	they come
volere	to want	voglio	vogliono	they want

* Notice that *sono* is the form used for both 'I am' and 'they are'.

XXXVII *Che succede?* 'What is happening?' Complete these sentences.

a I signori Pacelli _____ fare spese. (volere)
b _____ una macchina nuova. (avere)
c _____ all'ipermercato. (andare)
d _____ la macchina nel parcheggio. (lasciare)
e _____ spese. (fare)

f _____ dall'ipermercato. (uscire)
g Non _____ a ritrovare la loro macchina. (riuscire)
h La _____ dappertutto. (cercare)
i Non la _____ da nessuna parte. (vedere)
j _____ chiamare la polizia. (dovere)

D *Loro* and reflexive verbs

The reflexive pronoun for the *loro* form is *si*.

The reflexive form of ordinary verbs is often used to describe an action for which there is no known subject:
Si coltivano i limoni a Sorrento.   Lemons are cultivated in Sorrento.

Infinitive	Meaning	Third person pl.	Meaning
addormentarsi	to fall asleep	si addormentano	they fall asleep
alzarsi	to get up	si alzano	they get up
annoiarsi	to get bored	si annoiano	they get bored
arrabbiarsi	to get angry	si arrabbiano	they get angry
chiamarsi	to be called	si chiamano	they are called
farsi la barba	to shave	si fanno la barba	they shave
lavarsi	to wash (oneself)	si lavano	they wash (themselves)
pettinarsi	to comb one's hair	si pettinano	they comb their hair
riposarsi	to rest	si riposano	they rest
sedersi	to sit down	si siedono	they sit down
svegliarsi	to wake up	si svegliano	they wake up
vestirsi	to get dressed	si vestono	they get dressed

XXXVIII   Che fanno Francesca e Vittoria prima di uscire?

a (Loro) _____ (riposarsi)
b _____ alle sei. (svegliarsi)
c _____ (alzarsi)
d _____ (lavarsi)
e _____ (prepararsi) a uscire.
f _____ alle otto. (uscire)
g _____ al bar. (andare)
h I loro amici non _____ (arrivare)
i Le ragazze _____ (annoiarsi)
j _____ (andarsene*)

* This expression means 'to go away'; use the verb as normal, but place *ne* between the reflexive pronoun (*se* in this case) and the verb.

E Asking whether somebody else likes something (plural)

As before, the Italian way of expressing 'to like' uses 'to please' with the appropriate pronoun in front of it to express the person liking.

Gli piace Venezia? Do they like Venice? Does Venice please them?

So, for a plural thing liked, the verb becomes *piacciono*:

Sì, gli piacciono i canali. Yes, they like the canals. The canals please them.

Checklist: the *loro* form

You use the loro form when you are talking about someone or something.

The *loro* form always ends in *-no.*

The *loro* form of regular *-are* verbs is made by adding *-ano* to the stem.

The *loro* form of regular *-ere* and *-ire* verbs is made by adding *-ono* to the stem.

The most common irregular verbs are *andare* (*vanno*), *avere* (*hanno*), *essere* (*sono*) and *fare* (*fanno*).

The reflexive pronoun for the *loro* form is *si*: come *si chiamano?*

1.2.8 ▶**Fast track:** the present tense

Italian verbs change the spelling of their endings according to the person who is doing the action.

Remember that because each ending sounds different, the person word is not usually needed.

There are a few irregular verbs, some of which are useful everyday verbs, but then you probably already know some of these.

A -*are* verbs

Most Italian verbs are *-are* verbs.

The regular endings for *-are* verbs are *-o; -i; -a; -iamo; -ate; -ano.*

All new verbs are *-are* verbs, e.g. *filmare.*

Most *-are* verbs are regular, i.e. they follow the same pattern.

B   *-ere* verbs

There are fewer *-ere* verbs.

The regular endings for *-ere* verbs are *-o; -i; -e; -iamo; -ete; -ono.*

Most *-ere* verbs are regular, i.e. they follow the same pattern.

C   *-ire* verbs

There are not so many *-ire* verbs.

The regular endings for *-ire* verbs are *-o; -i; -e; -iamo; -ite; -ono.*

Most *-ire* verbs are regular, i.e. they follow the same pattern.

Some *-ire* verbs add *-isc-* to the stem in all but the *noi* and *voi* forms.

> Try to remember a phrase which you might use, which includes a
> word which you are trying to remember, e.g.
>
> Parlo bene l'italiano.
> Beviamo sempre vino rosso.
> Preferiscono andare in Italia.

D   The present tense of common regular verbs

Parlare	*Vendere*	*Partire*	*Preferire*
parlo	vendo	parto	preferisco
parli	vendi	parti	preferisci
parla	vende	parte	preferisce
parliamo	vendiamo	partiamo	preferiamo
parlate	vendete	partite	preferite
parlano	vendono	partono	preferiscono

> Try to learn each set of forms by heart, remembering that these
> are the models for the overwhelming majority of Italian verbs.
> Try copying each set in large letters onto A4 paper, stick it on the
> wall and learn it while shaving, putting on make-up or washing
> up – the best times to learn things by heart!

E   The effect of pronunciation on some verb forms

Considerations of pronunciation often affect verb forms.

1. Verbs like *conoscere* and all the *-ire* verbs with *-isc-* stems
in some forms: the *loro* form and the *io* form have a hard
pronunciation of the *-c-*, not the '-*sh*-' sound of other
forms. Thus:

1 sing. io	2 sing. tu	3 sing. lui/lei/Lei	1 pl. noi	2 pl. voi	3 pl. loro/Loro
hard *c*	soft *sc* = 'sh'				hard *c*
conosco preferisco	conosci preferisci	conosce preferisce	conosciamo preferiamo	conoscete preferite	conoscono preferiscono

2. A handful of otherwise regular verbs need an *-h-* to protect the hard *-c-* or *-g-* of the stem when followed by the *-i-* of the *tu* and *noi* forms; here are two examples:

c+h	g+h
cercare	**pagare**
cerco	pago
cer**ch**i	pa**gh**i
cerca	paga
cer**ch**iamo	pa**gh**iamo
cercate	pagate
cercano	pagano

3. Most verbs with infinitives ending in *-iare* lose the *-i* in the *tu* and *noi* forms to avoid having double *-i-*; here are some useful verbs like this:

cominciare	lasciare	mangiare	studiare	viaggiare
comincio	lascio	mangio	studio	viaggio
cominci	lasci	mangi	studi	viaggi
comincia	lascia	mangia	studia	viaggia
cominciamo	lasciamo	mangiamo	studiamo	viaggiamo
cominciate	lasciate	mangiate	studiate	viaggiate
cominciano	lasciano	mangiano	studiano	viaggiano

F The present tense of common irregular verbs

Here are some of the most useful irregular verbs:

andare	avere	dovere	essere
vado	ho	devo/debbo	sono
vai	hai	devi	sei
va	ha	deve	è
andiamo	abbiamo	dobbiamo	siamo
andate	avete	dovete	siete
vanno	hanno	devono/debbono	sono

fare	potere	sapere	volere
faccio	posso	so	voglio
fai	puoi	sai	vuoi
fa	può	sa	vuole
facciamo	possiamo	sappiamo	vogliamo
fate	potete	sapete	volete
fanno	possono	sanno	vogliono

The following two behave mostly like -*are* verbs apart from the -*a*- in the *tu* form and the -*nn*- of the *loro* form:

dare	stare
do	sto
dai	stai
dà	sta
diamo	stiamo
date	state
danno	stanno

The following two have a 'simplified' infinitive form, but present tense forms with a more normal stem, which is slightly variable in the case of *dire*:

bere	dire
bevo	dico
bevi	dici
beve	dice
beviamo	diciamo
bevete	dite
bevono	dicono

The following verbs have an irregular 'reinforced sound' in the *io* and *loro* forms, and/or a stem vowel change in some of the others: can you spot the patterns?

rimanere	tenere	venire	sedere
riman**g**o	ten**g**o	ven**g**o	s**ie**do
rimani	ti**e**ni	vi**e**ni	s**ie**di
rimane	ti**e**ne	vi**e**ne	s**ie**de
rimaniamo	teniamo	veniamo	sediamo
rimanete	tenete	venite	sedete
rimano	ten**g**ono	ven**g**ono	s**ie**dono

All verbs based on the verbs listed, but with a modifying prefix, perform in the same way as the 'base' verb whether it is regular or irregular, e.g.: *ripartire – partire; ritenere – tenere; disconoscere – conoscere; svenire – venire.*

XXXIX You are talking about yourself. Use the verbs in brackets.

a (Io) _____ una riunione con un collega. (avere)
b _____ pronto/a per partire. (essere)
c _____ in centro. (andare)
d _____ il metrò. (prendere)
e _____ alla stazione del Colosseo. (scendere)
f _____ dal metrò. (uscire)
g _____ la piazza. (attraversare)
h _____ il mio collega davanti al Colosseo. (aspettare)
i Non _____ aspettare molto tempo. (volere)
j Dopo mezz'ora _____ in albergo. (tornare)

XL Still using the same sentences, ask someone you know really well the same things. Use the *tu* form. For example:

Hai una riunione (tu)? (avere)

a _____ una riunione con un collega (tu)? (avere)
b _____ pronto/a per partire? (essere)
c _____ in centro? (andare)
d _____ il metrò? (prendere)
e _____ alla stazione del Colosseo? (scendere)
f _____ dal metrò? (uscire)
g _____ la piazza? (attraversare)
h _____ il tuo collega davanti al Colosseo? (aspettare)
i Non _____ aspettare molto tempo? (volere)
j Quando _____ in albergo? (tornare)

XLI Now report back in the singular, saying he/she does it. Choose the correct verb in the brackets. For example:

(lui/lei) Ha una riunione con un collega. (avere)

a (lui/lei) _____ una riunione con un collega. (ha/è/sale)
b _____ pronto/a per partire. (mette/è/sa)
c _____ in centro. (va/è/vende)
d _____ il metrò. (prende/sale/compra)
e _____ alla stazione del Colosseo. (scende/prende/dà)
f _____ dal metrò. (esce/sa/entra)
g _____ la piazza. (lavora/corre/attraversa)
h _____ il suo collega davanti al Colosseo. (ascolta/beve/aspetta)
i Non _____ aspettare molto tempo. (arriva/vuole/viene)
j Dopo mezz'ora _____ in albergo. (vuole/fa/torna)

XLII Now you are talking about yourself and a partner. Say 'we do' (or 'don't do') the same things. For example:

Noi abbiamo una riunione ....

a (Noi) _____ una riunione con un collega.
b _____ pronti/e per partire.
c _____ in centro.
d _____ il metrò.
e _____ alla stazione del Colosseo.
f _____ dal metrò.
g _____ la piazza.
h _____ il nostro collega davanti al Colosseo.
i Non _____ aspettare molto tempo.
j Dopo mezz'ora _____ in albergo.

XLIII Using the same sentences, ask someone else the same things. Use the *voi* form. For example:

Avete una riunione?

a _____ una riunione (voi)? (avere)
b _____ pronti/e? (essere)
c _____ in centro? (andare)
d _____ il metrò? (prendere)
e _____ alla stazione del Colosseo? (scendere)
f _____ dal metrò? (uscire)
g _____ la piazza? (attraversare)
h _____ il vostro collega davanti al Colosseo? (aspettare)
i Non _____ aspettare molto tempo? (volere)
j Quando _____ in albergo? (tornare)

XLIV Finally, say it in the plural: 'they do it'. Choose the correct verb. For example:

(Loro) hanno una riunione.

a (Loro) _____ una riunione con un collega. (hanno/salgono/stanno)
b _____ pronti/e. (sono/stanno/salgono)
c _____ in centro. (vanno/mettono/valgono)
d _____ il metrò. (prendono/conoscono/salgono)
e _____ alla stazione del Colosseo. (scendono/stanno/danno)
f _____ dal metrò. (escono/salgono/comprano)
g _____ la piazza. (ascoltano/guardano/attraversano)
h _____ il loro collega davanti al Colosseo. (lavorano/corrono/ aspettano)
i Non _____ aspettare molto tempo. (scelgono/vogliono/capiscono)
j Dopo mezz'ora _____ in albergo. (tornano/possono/hanno)

1.3 Negatives, interrogatives and imperatives

▶▶ **If you know what these are go on to 1.3.1.**

The negative is used to say 'no', you 'don't' do something, you 'haven't' got something, or to tell someone not to do something. A negative sentence is a sentence with a 'no' 'not' or 'don't' in it.

The interrogative is used to ask questions.

The imperative is used to give orders, directions or instructions – to tell someone what to do or what not to do.

1.3.1 Negatives: how to say what you don't do

▶▶ **If you know how to use *no* and *non* ..., go on to 1.3.2.**

To say you don't do something, you put *non* in front of the verb.

Non so.   I don't know.

If you wish to start the sentence with an 'introductory' negation, use *no*.

No, non parto.   No, I'm not leaving.

I Say you/they don't do these things by putting *non* in front of the verb. Say the sentences aloud to get used to the sound.

a They don't drink wine.   _____ vino. (bere)
b I don't often write letters.   _____ lettere spesso. (scrivere)
c She doesn't read her e-mails.   _____ la sua posta elettronica. (leggere)
d We don't buy magazines.   _____ riviste. (comprare)
e I don't know!   _____! (sapere)
f He can't find the entrance.   _____ a trovare l'ingresso. (riuscire)
g They are not coming tonight.   _____ questa sera. (venire)
h I don't want to go.   _____ andare. (volere)
i We don't like going there.   _____ andare lì. (piacere.... attenzione!)
j You don't eat garlic!   _____ l'aglio! (mangiare – tu)

1.3.2 Interrogatives: asking questions

There are four ways of asking a question. You can:

i   make a statement and change the intonation;
ii invert the subject and the verb where a subject pronoun is actually used;
iii use a question word, and then the verb as normal;

iv use a question word and invert the subject and verb
   where a subject pronoun is used.

In the following sections, read the examples and then cover
up the English and see if you understand the meanings;
then cover up the Italian and see if you can put them back
into Italian.

A Changing the intonation

This is the easiest and most used way to ask a question.
Remember you have to use a rising tone towards the end of
the question, which is what identifies a question when
spoken. Practise saying them aloud.

Capisci?	You understand?
Parla inglese?	You speak English?
Conoscete l'Albergo Salerno?	You know the Hotel Salerno?
Michele sa il latino?	Michele knows Latin?
Questo treno va a Cosenza?	This train is going to Cosenza?

B Inverting the subject and the verb

This can be done where the subject pronoun is used for
extra emphasis, being most common with *tu* and *Lei*. It can
be used where a name or noun is expressed as the subject:

Capisci tu?	Do you understand?
Parla inglese Lei?	Do you speak English?
Conoscete l'Albergo Salerno voi?	Do you know the Hotel Salerno?
Sa il latino Michele?	Does Michele know Latin?
Va a Bologna questo treno?	Is this train going to Bologna?

C Using a question word followed by the verb as normal

Che dici?	What are you saying?
Perché fa così?	Why are you doing this?
Dove alloggiate?	Where are you staying?
Come vanno a Palermo?	How are they going to Palermo?
Chi conoscete?	Whom do you know?
Quanti euro avete?	How many euros do you have?
Il treno quando arriva a Bologna?	When does the train arrive in Bologna?

D Using a question word and inverting the subject and verb

Che dici tu?	What are you saying?
Perché fa così Lei?	Why are you doing this?
Dove alloggiate voi?	Where are you staying?
Come vanno loro a Palermo?	How are they going to Palermo?
Chi conoscete voi?	Whom do you know?
Quanti euro avete voi?	How many euros do you have?
Quando arriva il treno a Bologna?	When does the train arrive at Bologna?

II Use method B to turn these statements into questions:

a I signori Bianchi abitano   Abitano a Brescia i signori
     a Brescia.   Bianchi?
b Vanno in vacanza.
c Prendono il treno.
d Vanno alla Costa Amalfitana.
e Hanno un appartamento lì.
f Affittano una macchina.
g Giocano a golf.
h Praticano lo sci acquatico.
i Hanno degli amici a Positano.
j La sera cenano in un ristorante.

Remember that pronouns are not often used except where
extra emphasis needs to be put on the person involved.

III Use method D with these question words:

a Where are they going?   Dove _____ ? (andare)
                                     Dove vanno loro?
b When are they leaving?   Quando _____ ? (partire)
c How are they travelling?   Come _____ ? (viaggiare)
d Why are they in Bari?   Perché _____ a Bari? (stare)
e What are they doing?   Che _____ ? (fare)
f Who are they meeting?   Con chi _____ una riunione?
                                     (avere)
g How long are they staying   Quanto tempo _____ in albergo?
     at the hotel?   (stare)

1.3.3 Imperatives: giving orders, directions or instructions

▶▶   **If you know how to give orders and instructions go
on to fast track 1.3.4.**

The imperative is the part of the verb you use when you are
telling someone to do something, or giving instructions or
an order: 'Watch out! Stop! Turn left!' etc.

In Italian, since there are four ways of saying 'you', there
are four ways of telling somebody what to do. Of course,
you use the *tu* form only when speaking to someone you
know well or someone younger than you, the *voi* form for
two or more of them; you use the *Lei* form for a stranger or
somebody senior to you, and the *Loro* form for two or more
of them, but this is used in very formal circumstances only.

IV Look at these examples. Some are for *tu*, some for *Lei* and
others for *voi*. You will probably have heard some of these
before. Which ones do you know already? They are
jumbled – can you sort them out?

a Come on!	Ascoltate!
b Go!	Fai presto!
c Do sit down!	Aspetta!
d Turn left!	Resti in linea!
e Listen!	Si accomodi!
f Wait!	Dai!
g Hold the line (telephone).	Va'!
h Hurry up!	Giri a sinistra!

A   Giving a relative or friend advice or instructions using the *tu* form

The *tu* form of address is used to give advice, instructions and orders to family members or friends. A special form of the verb is used for this (the imperative); this is easy to form: for -*are* verbs, it ends in -*a*, and for -*ere* and -*ire* verbs it is the normal *tu* form.

Compra una cravatta nuova!	Buy a new tie!
Bevi il vino del Veneto!	Drink wine from the Venice region!
Sali facendo attenzione!	Get in carefully!

Note that in the case of reflexive verbs, the reflexive pronoun is added to the end of the imperative:

Alzati!	Get up!
Siediti qui!	Sit here!
Lasciami in pace!	Leave me in peace!

Some irregular verbs have a special stem, but most useful verbs present no problems.

Infinitive	Meaning	*tu* imperative	Meaning
andare	to go	va'/vai	go
avere	to have	abbi	have
dare	to give	da'/dai	give
dire	to say	di'	say
essere	to be	sii	be
fare	to do/make	fa'/fai	do/make
sapere	to know	sappi	know
stare	to stand, be	sta'/stai	be/stand

Note that when *da'*, *di'*, *fa'*, *sta'* and *va'* are followed by a pronoun other than *gli*, the first consonant of the pronoun is doubled.

Dammi la mano!	Give me your hand!
Fagli un caffè!	Make him a coffee!

To give negative commands with *tu*, simply use *non* followed by the infinitive of the verb.

Non gridare!			Don't shout!
Non mangiare questo!			Don't eat that!
Non ti preoccupare!	or	Non preoccuparti!	Don't worry!
Non mi lasciare!	or	Non lasciarmi!	Don't leave me!

Note how pronouns go in front of the negative imperative or on the end of it.

V Tell a friend or relative to do or not to do these things:

a Shut up! _____ zitto! (stare)
b Don't sit down! Non _____! (sedersi)
c Be careful! _____ attenzione! (fare)
d Give me a pen! _____ mi una penna! (dare)
e Be good! _____ il bravo! (fare)
f Don't come here! Non _____ qui! (venire)
g Get out of here! _____ via! (andare)
h Get up! _____ ! (alzarsi: add reflexive pronoun to end)

B Giving relatives or friends advice or instructions using the *voi* form

For *voi* imperatives when speaking to two or more children, family members, or friends, use the normal *voi* form of the present tense, which is usually like the infinitive, but ending in *-te* instead of *-re*.

Aspettate!	Wait!
Andate!	Go!
Venite subito!	Come quick!

This form is also used for negative *voi* imperatives:

Non mi dimenticate!	Don't forget me!
Non bevete quello!	Don't drink that!
Non scendete la scala!	Don't go down the stairs!

C Giving a stranger advice or instructions using the *Lei* form

The *Lei* form of address is the one most likely to be used to give advice, instructions and orders to strangers or in public places. A special form of the verb is used for this imperative (the subjunctive); this is easy to form, adding *-i* to the stem of *-are* verbs, and *-a* to the stem of *-ere* and *-ire* verbs. The same verb form is used for negative commands:

Beva più acqua!	Drink more water!
Salga facendo attenzione!	Get in carefully!
Non compri questa macchina!	Don't buy this car!

Some irregular verbs have a special stem which you will recognise from the present tense, and any spelling changes seen in certain verbs are also applied in this imperative form.

Note that reflexive and other pronouns are *not* added to the end of the imperative verb form this time but are placed in front of it:

La beva!   Drink it!
Non la compri!   Don't buy it!

Here are some examples of *Lei* forms for regular, spelling-change and useful irregular verbs, and a reflexive verb (*sedersi*):

Infinitive	Meaning	*Lei* command form	Meaning
parlare	to speak	parli	speak!
vendere	to sell	venda	sell!
partire	to leave	parta	leave!
finire	to finish	finisca	finish!
cercare	to look for	cerchi	look for!
pagare	to pay	paghi	pay!
andare	to go	vada	go!
bere	to drink	beva	drink!
dare	to give	dia	give!
dire	to say/tell	dica	say/tell!
essere	to be	sia	be!
fare	to do	faccia	do!
rimanere	to stay	rimanga	stay!
salire	to go up	salga	go up!
sapere	to know	sappia	know!
scegliere	to choose	scelga	choose!
stare	to stand, be	stia	stand, be!
uscire	to go out	esca	go out!
venire	to come	venga	come!
sedersi	to sit down	si sieda	sit down!

In public notices, and in instructions such as for recipes, the infinitive is often used in place of imperatives:

Spingere   Push (on a door)
Suonare   Ring (on a doorbell)
Tagliare i pomodori   Chop up the tomatoes
Non calpestare l'erba   Don't walk on the grass

VI   What do these mean? Pair the jumbled phrases correctly:

a Enter your PIN.	Per favore, rimanga in linea.
b Pull.	Spingere.
c Wait for the tone.	Parli vicino al microfono.
d Speak into the microphone.	Timbri il biglietto.
e Sign here.	Inserire il numero di codice segreto.
f Cancel your ticket.	Senta, per favore.
g Push.	Prema il pulsante.
h Please hold the line.	Dica.
i Wait.	Firmi qui.
j Press the button.	Tirare.
k Listen, please.	Aspetti il segnale di libero.
l Hello. (tell me – e.g. answering phone)	Aspetti.

Tick the ones you know already. Highlight any which are different from what you would have expected and choose three new ones to try to remember.

VII   Your assistant is not well. Give him/her some advice using the *Lei* form of the imperative.

a Sit down a minute.	Si _____ un momento. (sedere)
b Go to see the doctor.	_____ dal medico. (andare)
c Drink more water.	_____ più acqua. (bere)
d Eat more fruit.	_____ più frutta. (mangiare)
e Walk to work every day.	_____ a piedi al lavoro ogni giorno. (venire)
f Smoke less.	_____ di meno. (fumare)
g Go jogging.	_____ un po' di footing. (fare)
h Get some fresh air.	_____ un po' d'aria fresca. (prendere)
i Go to bed earlier.	_____ a letto più presto. (andare)
j Sleep longer.	_____ di più. (dormire)

D   Giving strangers advice or instructions using the *Loro* form

The *Loro* form of address is the plural one most likely to be used to give advice, instructions and orders to strangers or in public places in very formal circumstances. A special form of the verb is used for this imperative (the subjunctive); this is easy to form, adding *-ino* to the stem of *-are* verbs, and *-ano* to the stem of *-ere* and *-ire* verbs; in other words, it has *-no* added to the end like the *Loro* form.

Make your way to the restaurant!	Si accomodino al ristorante!
Try this new wine!	Assaggino questo vino nuovo!
Fill in this form!	Compilino questo modulo!

As before, irregularities and spelling changes in the verb stem apply to this form too. Note also that reflexive pronouns and other pronouns are placed in front of the *Loro* imperative.

to sit down sedersi – Si siedano! Sit down!

This same form of the verb is used for giving negative commands, although these are rather rare:

Non si preoccupino!   Don't worry!
Non mangino in questo ristorante!   Don't eat at this restaurant!

VIII Fill in the gaps in the table below showing both regular and irregular examples. Highlight any which are different from what you would have expected and choose three new ones to try to remember.

Infinitive	Meaning	*Lei* command form	*Loro* command form	Meaning
_____	to speak	parli	parlino	speak!
vendere	_____	venda	vendano	sell!
partire	to leave	parta	_____	leave!
_____	to finish	finisca	finiscano	finish!
cercare	to look for	cerchi	cerchino	_____
pagare	_____	paghi	paghino	pay!
andare	to go	vada	_____	go!
bere	_____	beva	bevano	drink!
dare	to give	_____	diano	give!
dire	to say/tell	dica	dicano	_____
essere	_____	sia	siano	be!
_____	to do	faccia	facciano	do!
rimanere	_____	rimanga	rimangano	stay!
salire	to go up	_____	salgano	go up!
sapere	to know	sappia	_____	know!
scegliere	to choose	scelga	scelgano	choose!
_____	to stay, be	stia	stiano	stay, be!
uscire	to go out	_____	escano	go out!
venire	_____	venga	vengano	come!
sedersi	to sit down	si sieda	si siedano	sit down!

E   The *noi* imperative

As in English, there is a way of saying 'Let's do' in Italian. In fact, this is the subjunctive *noi* form, which is identical to the normal form. As a reminder, here are the forms for regular verbs, a couple of spelling-change verbs, two useful irregular verbs and a reflexive verb; note that reflexive pronouns are added to the end of the imperative.

Infinitive	Meaning	*Noi* imperative	Meaning
comprare	to buy	compriamo!	let's buy
vendere	to sell	vendiamo!	let's sell
partire	to leave	partiamo!	let's leave
finire	to finish	finiamo!	let's finish
cercare	to look for	cerchiamo!	let's look for
pagare	to pay	paghiamo!	let's pay
andare	to go	andiamo!	let's go
fare	to do/make	facciamo!	let's do/make
sedersi	to sit down	sediamoci!	let's sit down

IX How would you say:

a Let's go out.
b Let's stay at home.
c Let's watch TV.
d Let's eat.
e Let's get up.

X How would you give these instructions? If you are likely to need to use the *tu* form (*Mangia la verdura!, Va' a letto!*) practise this form; otherwise concentrate on the *Lei* form. Both sets of answers are given.

a _____ a sinistra! (girare)
b _____ la scala! (salire)
c _____ la prima strada a destra! (prendere)
d _____ sempre diritto! (andare)
e _____ fino al prossimo semaforo! (continuare)
f _____ a sinistra e a destra! (guardare)
g _____ la strada! (attraversare)
h _____ l'autobus! (prendere)
i _____ davanti al teatro! (scendere)
j _____ (mi) un messaggio quando arrivi! (mandare)

XI How would you tell someone to do these things? Use the *Lei* form.

a Spend less time watching TV. _____ meno tempo a guardare la TV. (passare)
b Eat more vegetables. _____ più verdura. (mangiare)
c Drink more water. _____ più acqua. (bere)
d Go jogging. _____ footing. (fare)
e Close the door. _____ la porta. (chiudere)
f Open the window. _____ la finestra. (aprire)
g Show your passport. _____ il passaporto. (far vedere)
h Speak more slowly. _____ più lentamente. (parlare)
i Come with me. _____ con me. (venire)

XII Let's try a keep-fit session. Give the *voi* form of the verb in brackets, taking particular care with reflexives.

    a Come in!   _____ (entrare)

    b Get in line.   _____ in fila. (mettersi)

    c Find a space.   _____ uno spazio. (trovare)

    d Run to the wall.   _____ fino alla parete. (correre)

    e Stand with your feet apart.   _____ con i piedi divaricati. (stare)

    f Stretch your arms.   _____ le braccia. (allungare)

    g Do five press-ups.   _____ cinque flessioni sulle braccia. (fare)

    h Lower your shoulders.   _____ le spalle. (abbassare)

    i Bend your knees.   _____ le ginocchia. (flettare)

    j Don't move!   Non _____! (muoversi)

XIII Tell some Italian visitors the way to the town hall, using the *Loro* form.

    a Prima, _____ di qui. (uscire)

    b _____ a destra. (girare)

    c _____ la seconda strada a destra. (prendere)

    d _____ sempre diritto. (andare)

    e _____ la piazza. (attraversare)

    f _____ la strada fino alla rotatoria. (seguire)

    g _____ a destra: il municipio è lì di fronte. (girare)

XIV First match the English and Italian, then cover up the right-hand side of the page and see if you can remember the Italian.

    a Don't open the door. (tu)   Non aspettate qui.

    b Don't walk on the grass. (voi)   Non beva l'acqua.

    c Don't eat in the shop. (voi)   Non vestirti di nero.

    d Don't drink the water. (Lei)   Non lasciare i bagagli qui.

    e Don't cross the road here. (voi)   Non aprire la porta.

    f Don't lean out of the window. (Loro)   Non mangiate nel negozio.

    g Don't leave your luggage here. (tu)   Non calpestate l'erba.

    h Don't wait here. (voi)   Non fumino.

    i Don't put your boots on the table. (Lei)   Non sporgetevi dal finestrino.

    j Don't wear black. (tu)   Non metta gli stivali sul tavolo.

    k Don't smoke. (Loro)   Non attraversate la strada qui.

XV These recipe instructions are for an Italian Easter *frittata* (omelette). Here they are expressed with infinitives. Put them into the *tu* form.

a	Prepare the ingredients.	Preparare gli ingredienti.
b	Chop up the salami and bacon.	Tagliare a pezzetti il salame e la pancetta.
c	Fry the bacon and then the salami a little.	Friggere un po' la pancetta e poi il salame.
d	Beat the eggs into a bowl.	Battere le uova in una terrina.
e	Add the salami and bacon.	Aggiungere il salame e la pancetta.
f	Put the chopped parsley into the bowl.	Mettere nella terrina il prezzemolo tritato.
g	Mix well.	Mescolare bene.
h	Warm up a frying pan with some olive oil.	Riscaldare un po' d'olio d'oliva in una padella.
i	Pour the mixture into the pan.	Versare il contenuto della terrina nella padella.
j	Fry the omelette slowly.	Friggere a fuoco lento.
k	Turn the omelette over …	Girare la frittata …
l	… and fry the other side.	… e friggere l'altro lato.

1.3.4 ▶Fast track: negatives, interrogatives and imperatives

A Negatives: saying you don't do something
You put *non* in front of the verb.

Non so.	I don't know.
Non vende la sua macchina.	She/he isn't selling her/his car.

B Interrogatives: asking questions
You can:

- make a statement and change the intonation:

  Vai a Massa? — Are you going to Massa?

- invert the subject and the verb when you want to stress the subject:

  Va lei a Massa? — Is **she** going to Massa?

- use a question word, then the verb as normal:

  Dove andate? — Where are you going?

- use a question word, then invert the expressed subject and verb when you want to stress the subject:

  Dove vanno loro? — Where are **they** going?

Useful question words:

Quanto/a/i/e?	How much?/How many?
Come?	How? Pardon?

Dove?	Where?
Perché?	Why?
Quando?	When?
Che/Che cosa/Cosa?	What?
Chi?	Who?
Quale/i?	Which?

C Imperatives: giving orders, directions and instructions

To make the imperative when talking to children, family and friends, you use a form ending in -*a* for -*are* verbs, and -*i* for -*ere* and -*ire* verbs. For most verbs, the stem is taken from the infinitive. Some verbs have spelling changes or are irregular.

| Aspetta! | Wait! |

For *noi* imperatives, use the normal *noi* form, which is usually like the infinitive, but ending in -*iamo* instead of -*re*.

| Aspettiamo! | Let's wait! |
| Andiamo | Let's go! |

For *voi* imperatives when speaking to two or more people, family members or friends, use the normal *voi* form, which is usually like the infinitive, but ending in -*te* instead of -*re*.

| Aspettate! | Wait! |

To make the *Lei* imperative when talking to strangers or seniors, you use the appropriate form of the subjunctive, which for -*are* verbs ends in -*i*, and for -*ere* and -*ire* verbs ends in -*a*. For most verbs, the stem is taken from the infinitive, and some verbs have spelling changes or irregularities.

| Aspetti! | Wait! |

For the *Loro* imperative when talking to two or more strangers or seniors, you use the *loro* form of the subjunctive which for -*are* verbs ends in -*ino*, and for -*ere* and -*ire* verbs ends in -*ano*. For most verbs, the stem is taken from the infinitive, but some verbs have spelling changes or irregularities. This form of the imperative is used rarely and in formal circumstances.

| Aspettino! | Wait! |

Note that pronouns are added to the end of the imperative.

| Aspettami! | Wait for me! |

To give negative commands with *tu*, use *non* followed by the infinitive of the verb. For all other negative commands, put *non* in front of the positive forms.

1.4 The past tenses

Saying what you have done or what has happened

▶▶ **If you know when to use the perfect and imperfect tenses go on to 1.4.1.**

In Italian, just as in English, there are different ways of expressing the past. The tenses you will need to use most are the perfect tense and the imperfect.

A The perfect tense: *il passato prossimo*

The perfect tense is so called because it describes a single, completed action; like the English equivalent, it is mostly used for an action in the immediate past, one which has just happened, but it is also used for the English past simple, as seen in the examples below. In some ways it is the easiest Italian tense, but it does have its complications, which have to be learnt.

I have eaten/I ate.   Ho mangiato.
I have arrived/I arrived.   Sono arrivato.

The perfect tense translates 'I have played' and 'I played', and the question forms 'Have you played?' and 'Did you play?'.

You use the perfect tense when you are talking or asking about something which happened and finished in the past.

 Ask yourself: Did it happen once in the past? Is it over? Is it finished? Then use the perfect tense.

B The imperfect tense: *l'imperfetto*

The imperfect tense translates 'I was playing when ...,' 'Were you playing when ...?' and 'I used to play (a long time ago)', and is used for repeated actions and descriptions in the past.

You use the imperfect tense:

• to talk about what used to happen in general:
I used to go to school by bus.   Andavo a scuola in autobus.

• to describe things in the past:
It was always raining.   Pioveva sempre.

• to say what was happening when something else happened (an interrupted action).
I was having a shower when   Mi facevo la doccia quando è
  he arrived.   arrivato.

Note how in the last one the single completed action is described in the perfect.

 Ask yourself: Did it happen once in the past? Is it over? Is it finished? Then use the perfect tense.

 Ask yourself: Is it something which used to happen in the past? Was it happening when something else happened? If you can use 'was/were' + an -ing form in English, you use the imperfect in Italian.

C   The past definite tense: *il passato remoto*

The past definite tense, so called because it describes a single, completed action at a defined moment in the (not recent) past; like the English equivalent – the past simple – it is mostly used for an action in the distant past. It is mostly used nowadays in legal language and in narrative or historical Italian, but you may come across it occasionally in spoken form: it is regularly used in spoken Italian in certain regions, mainly in the South but also in Tuscany and Emilia Romagna. In the rest of Italy, the perfect tense is used instead.

My parents were born in Italy.	I miei genitori nacquero in Italia.
He sold his car.	Vendé la sua macchina.

I   Which tense are you going to use?

a Yesterday I went to town.
b I bought a new pair of trainers.
c Then I went to the gym.
d I used to go three times a week.
e I met my girlfriend at the gym.
f She was on the rowing machine.
g I was doing weights.
h She was laughing at me.
i I asked her why.
j My shorts were inside out.

1.4.1   The perfect tense: *il passato prossimo*

▶▶   **If you know how to form the perfect tense with *avere* and *essere* go to 1.4.2.**

The perfect tense in Italian is made up of two parts like the English perfect tense: the appropriate part of an auxiliary verb – *avere* 'to have' or *essere* 'to be' – and the past participle. Remember, though, that it is used for both recent actions in the past and more distant ones. Most verbs form the perfect tense with *avere*, but some examples with *essere* follow.

A The perfect tense with avere

First, verbs which use *avere*; to get used to the sound of the perfect tense choose one of the phrases, or make up one of your own and practise saying it until you are really fluent. Study the following chart carefully.

Auxiliary verb	Past participle	avere	Participio Passato	Past simple meaning
I have	spoken	ho	parlato	I spoke
you have (familiar)	eaten	hai	mangiato	you ate
you have (formal), he/she has	sold	ha	venduto	you sold he/she sold
we have	understood	abbiamo	capito	we understood
you have (familiar pl.)	finished	avete	finito	you finished
you have (formal pl.), they have	preferred	hanno	preferito	you preferred they preferred

You can see that the past participles are formed as follows:

-are verbs	-ato
-ere verbs	-uto
-ire verbs	-ito

Here are some examples of *avere* verbs in sentences:

Ho chiesto una birra.	I ordered a beer.
Hai fatto lo shopping.	You did the shopping.
Ha perso un coltello e ha rotto una tazza.	She has lost a knife and broken a cup.
Abbiamo preso il treno delle sei.	We got the 6 o'clock train.
Avete dimenticato le chiavi.	You have forgotten the keys.
Hanno abbandonato la macchina.	They have abandoned the car.

II Practise with the following. How would you say:

a I have spoken   _____ parlato

b you have spoken (tu)   _____

c she has spoken   _____

d they have spoken   _____

e you have sold (Loro)   _____ venduto

f we have sold   _____

g have you sold? (voi)   _____

h John has understood   _____ capito

i you have understood (Lei)   _____

j (my wife and I) have understood _____

III Who watched the *Telegiornale* news bulletin? Complete these sentences by adding the right form of *avere*.

a (Noi) _____ guardato il Telegiornale delle 10:00.
b (Loro) _____ guardato il Telegiornale delle 12:00.
c (Lei) _____ guardato il Telegiornale delle 14:00.
d Bianca_____ guardato il Telegiornale delle 16:00.
e (Voi) _____ guardato il Telegiornale delle 18:00.
f (Loro) _____ guardato il Telegiornale delle 20:00.
g (Tu) _____ guardato il Telegiornale delle 22:00.
h (Io) _____ guardato il Telegiornale delle 24:00.
i (Luigi) _____ guardato il Telegiornale delle 02:00.
j (Lei) _____ guardato il Telegiornale delle 04:00.

B The perfect tense with *essere*

In Italian, as we have seen, some verbs form the perfect with *essere* instead of *avere*. These include *all* reflexive verbs, of which there are a couple of examples in this table.

Auxiliary verb (English version)	Past participle	*essere*	*Participio Passato*	Past simple meaning
I have	gone	sono	andato/a	I went
you have (familiar)	entered	sei	entrato/a	you entered
you have (formal), he/she has	fallen	è	caduto/a	you fell he/she fell
we have	gone out	siamo	usciti/e	we went out
you have (familiar pl.)	gone up	siete	saliti/e	you went up
you have (formal pl.), they have	left	sono	partiti/e	you left they left
I have	washed myself	mi sono	lavato/a	I washed myself
you have	got up	vi siete	alzati/e	you got up

You can see that with *essere* verbs the past participles behave like adjectives and agree in number and gender with the subject; thus, with singular subjects they end in -*o* for masculine and -*a* for feminine subjects. In the plural they end in -*i* for masculines and -*e* for feminines. (For noun endings and adjective agreement, see 2.1 and 4.1.1).

C Verbs which use *essere* to form the perfect tense

The majority of intransitive verbs (ones which do not normally have an object) and reflexive verbs form the perfect tense with *essere*. Here are some examples from the main groups of such verbs:

- most verbs of movement or lack of movement:
  andare, arrivare, cadere, entrare, essere, fuggire, giungere, partire, restare, rimanere, salire, scappare, scendere, stare, tornare, uscire, venire

- verbs which indicate change:
  apparire, crescere, dimagrire, diventare, guarire, ingrassare, morire, nascere, svanire

- impersonal verbs and verbs describing the weather:
  avvenire, bastare, dispiacere, mancare, piacere, sembrare, nevicare, piovere

A few verbs can use either *avere* or *essere* depending on whether they are being used transitively or intransitively; with *dovere*, *potere* and *volere*, *essere* can be used if the following verb is an *essere* verb:

Non sono potuto andare al   I could not go to the cinema
   cinema con mio fratello.   with my brother.

Here are some examples of *essere* verbs in sentences:

Sono andato al bar.   I went to the bar.
Sei uscito/a alle due.   You went out at two o'clock.
Luisa si è alzata alle otto.   Luisa got up at eight o'clock.
Ci siamo riposati a casa.   We had a rest at home.
Siete tornati/e a Napoli.   You went back to Naples.
Loro sono partiti/e per Roma.   They left for Rome.

IV Complete these sentences by selecting the correct form of the past participle. Then try translating them into English.

a Michele è andato/andata/andati al lavoro.
b Maria Grazia è tornato/tornata/tornate a casa.
c E tu, Francesca, a che ora sei arrivate/arrivata/arrivati a scuola?
d I ragazzi sono già uscite/uscito/usciti.
e Emanuele e Alberto, a che ora vi siete alzati/alzate/alzato?
f Le mie amiche italiane sono venuti/venute/venuta a trovarmi.

V Put the verbs in these sentences into the correct form; don't forget the agreements.

a Franco _____ alle dieci. (arrivare)
b Laura _____ alle sette. (svegliarsi)
c Noi _____ per Genova alle undici. (partire)
d Loro _____ molto a Capri. (divertirsi)
e Gianni e Rosaria _____ a Ercolano. (andare)
f Lei _____ a trovarmi a casa. (venire)

To make the perfect tense you use the right person of *avere* 'to have' or *essere* 'to be' + the past participle:

avere: ho, hai, ha, abbiamo, avete, hanno
essere: sono, sei, è, siamo, siete, sono

1.4.2 How to form the past participle

▶▶ **If you know how to form the past participle, go to 1.4.3.**

A Regular verbs

In English the past participle of regular verbs is formed by adding 'ed' to the infinitive:

play   played   watch   watched   dance   danced

In Italian, *-are, -ere* and *-ire* verbs each form their past participles in different ways.

-*are* verbs	-*ere* verbs	-*ire* verbs
-ato	-uto	-ito

You take off the ending *-are, -ere* or *-ire* and add *-ato, -uto, -ito*: *parlare > parlato; vendere > venduto; partire > partito*.

VI Using these rules, what would be the past participles of these verbs?

a giocare		**k** lavare
b mangiare		**l** rivendere
c finire		**m** fermare
d vendere		**n** potere
e ascoltare		**o** tirare
f ripetere		**p** dimenticare
g tenere		**q** uscire
h aspettare		**r** entrare
i sistemare		**s** sentire
j invitare		**t** partire

B Agreement of past participles

You have found in section 1.4.1 that with verbs which use *essere* for the perfect tense, the past participle has to match the subject in number and gender. With *avere* verbs, the past participle has to agree with the direct object pronouns *lo, la, li, le* which go in front of the verb. You will sometimes see this agreement in other situations with *avere* verbs, but these types of agreement are mostly optional, so there is no need to worry about them. Here are some examples of necessary agreements:

Dov'è la mia penna? La ho/L'ho dimenticata.

Where is my pen? I have forgotten it.

Ti piacciono i gatti? Li ho comprati ieri.

Do you like the cats? I bought them yesterday.

Dove sono le ragazze? Non le ho viste.

Where are the girls? I haven't seen them.

VII *Che cosa ha fatto Marco stamattina?* 'What did Marco do this morning?' Add the right form of the past participle, and watch out for any past participle agreements.

a Ho _____ a tennis con Giulio.

I played tennis with Giulio. (giocare)

b Poi ho _____ mia moglie a pranzo.

Then I invited my wife to lunch. (invitare)

c Dopo ho _____ il mio collega Giorgio.

Next I rang my colleague Giorgio. (chiamare)

d Abbiamo _____ del nuovo progetto.

We talked about the new plan. (parlare)

e Mi ha _____ la sua cooperazione.

He assured me of his cooperation. (assicurare)

f Abbiamo _____ la data della conferenza stampa.

We considered the date of the press conference. (studiare)

g Mi ha _____ il nuovo dépliant per posta elettronica.

He sent me the new brochure by e-mail. (mandare)

h Ho _____ una pagina.

I changed a page. (cambiare)

i L'ho _____.

I printed it out. (stampare)

j Ecco i dépliant; li ho _____.

Here are the brochures; I printed them. (stampare)

k Le lettere? Le ho _____ io.

The letters? I sent them. (mandare)

l Dopo ho _____ una telenovela.

After that I watched a TV soap. (guardare)

C Irregular past participles

Many English past participles are irregular, but we are so used to them that we don't notice them.

run > run; eat > eaten; drink > drunk

Some Italian verbs also have irregular past participles. Although there seem to be quite a lot, they are easy to learn, as clusters of them follow similar patterns. Fortunately, *-are* verbs are all regular except for *fare > fatto*. Most *-ire* verbs are regular except for those grouped together in the chart below; some similar verbs are given – they follow the same pattern, but there are many others.

Remember that the examples can be translated as e.g. 'I have opened' or 'I opened':

Infinitive	Past participle	Example	Meaning	Similar
apparire	apparso	il sole è apparso	the sun appeared	scomparire
aprire	aperto	ho aperto la porta	I have opened the door	riaprire
coprire	coperto	ha coperto la padella	he covered the frying-pan	scoprire
dire	detto	non hanno detto niente	they have said nothing	maledire
morire	morto	mio zio è morto	my uncle has died	
offrire	offerto	abbiamo offerto 20 euro	we offered 20 euros	soffrire
venire	venuto	non è venuta oggi	she did not come today	avvenire

The following chart lists other important irregular past participles; they are grouped so that you can see which past participles are formed in similar ways. Remember, there are two ways of translating each one.

Infinitive	Past participle	Example	Meaning	Similar
essere	stato	sono stato a Salerno	I have been to Salerno	
nascere	nato	è nata a Bergamo	she was born in Bergamo	rinascere
bere	bevuto	hanno bevuto una birra	they drank a beer	
fare	fatto	ho fatto un errore	I made a mistake	soddisfare
rompere	rotto	hai rotto la chiave	you have broken the key	irrompere
costringere	costretto	mi ha costretto a farlo	he forced me to do it	
dirigere	diretto	Ponti ha diretto il film	Ponti directed the film	
distruggere	distrutto	avete distrutto la casa!	you've wrecked the house!	
friggere	fritto	ho fritto delle cipolle	I have fried some onions	
leggere	letto	hai letto questo libro?	have you read this book?	eleggere
scrivere	scritto	ha scritto una lettera	she wrote a letter	descrivere

Infinitive	Past participle	Example	Meaning	Similar
chiedere	chiesto	ho chiesto un aumento	I asked for a rise	richiedere
porre	posto	abbiamo posto le basi	we've laid the foundations	imporre
vedere	visto	avete visto un treno?	did you see a train?	rivedere
rimanere	rimasto	sono rimasti a casa	they stayed at home	
rispondere	risposto	hanno risposto ieri	they replied yesterday	
risolvere	risolto	ha risolto il problema?	did he solve the problem?	dissolvere
volgere	volto	ha volto le spalle	he turned his back	rivolgere
spingere	spinto	abbiamo spinto la porta	we pushed the door	respingere
vincere	vinto	hanno vinto la partita	they won the match	
conoscere	conosciuto	ho conosciuto Gigli	I met Gigli	riconoscere
piacere	piaciuto	mi è piaciuto molto	I liked him a lot	dispiacere
chiudere	chiuso	hanno chiuso la porta	they closed the door	socchiudere
decidere	deciso	avete deciso?	have you decided?	
prendere	preso	abbiamo preso un tè	we have had a tea	riprendere
ridere	riso	ha riso sotto i baffi	he laughed up his sleeve	sorridere
spendere	speso	hai speso una fortuna!	you have spent a fortune!	
mettere	messo	lo avete messo fuori	you have put him out	rimettere
muovere	mosso	ho mosso mari e monti!	I have moved heaven and earth!	rimuovere

Note that only a few of the similar 'compound' verbs are given as examples: there are very many others. Keep your eyes open!

VIII Complete these sentences by adding the past participle of the verb given in brackets.

a Il cliente ha _____ il nuovo dépliant. (vedere)

The customer has seen the new brochure.

b Noi abbiamo _____ il testo. (scrivere)

We wrote the text.

c Palma lo ha _____ nel computer. (immettere)

Palma put it on the computer.

d La ditta FoCo ha _____ questa versione. (fare)

The FoCo company made this version.

e Il cliente ha _____ che gli piace. (dire)

The customer said he liked it.

f Ha _____ il contratto subito! (chiedere)

He asked for the contract straight away.

IX Now tell the story of Salvo's car. Complete these sentences using the perfect tense of the verb given in brackets. Not all the past participles are irregular!

a Salvo _____ 100.000 euro nella lotteria. (vincere)

Salvo won 100,000 Euros in the lottery.

b _____ comprare una nuova auto per sua moglie. (volere)

He wanted to buy a new car for his wife.

c _____ lo spot di una macchina elettrica. (vedere)

He saw an advert for an electric car.

d _____ la macchina. (comprare)

He bought the car.

e L'auto non _____ a sua moglie. (piacere)

His wife didn't like the car.

f _____ di venderla. (decidere)

She decided to sell it.

g _____ un annuncio sul giornale. (mettere)

She put an advertisement in the newspaper.

h Un amico di suo marito _____ un appuntamento per provare l'auto. (prendere)

A friend of her husband made an appointment to try the car out.

i Salvo _____ sua moglie con il suo amico in macchina. (vedere)

Salvo saw his wife in the car with his friend.

j _____ che si trattava di un' avventura. (credere)

He thought they were having an affair.

k _____ la macchina. (seguire)

He followed the car.

l _____ a velocità eccessiva. (andare)

He went too fast.

m La Polizia Stradale l' _____ (fermare)

The police stopped him.

n _____ pagare una multa. (dovere)

He had to pay a fine.

X Now can you translate these?

a Sofia has read his latest novel (il suo ultimo romanzo).

b Have you read the book?

c We haven't read the book.
d They have seen the film of the book.
e Sofia saw the film yesterday.
f We haven't seen the film yet.
g Have you seen the film?

Checklist: past participles

Most past participles end in -*ato*, -*uto* or -*ito*.

Regular:

-*are* verbs end in -ato;
-*ere* verbs end in -uto;
-*ire* verbs end in -ito.

Many of the most commonly used verbs have irregular past participles:

Look for patterns to try to remember them:

aperto, coperto; detto, fatto; scritto, letto; posto, visto; deciso, preso.

1.4.3 Reflexive verbs in the perfect tense

Reflexive verbs behave the same in the perfect tense as in the present, with the reflexive pronoun before the appropriate part of the auxiliary verb *essere*. This means, of course that the past participles have to agree with the subject.

Present	Perfect
mi alzo	mi sono alzato/a
ti alzi	ti sei alzato/a
si alza	si è alzato/a
ci alziamo	ci siamo alzati/e
vi alzate	vi siete alzati/e
si alzano	si sono alzati/e

At first you will probably only need to use reflexive verbs in the first person, so learn one phrase by heart and use it as a model to make other phrases later.

mi sono alzato presto	I got up early
mi sono lavato	I got washed
mi sono pettinato	I combed my hair
mi sono preparato per andare al cinema	I got ready to go to the cinema

XI For more practice with the other persons, see if you can give the right form of the perfect tense of *alzarsi* to complete these sentences: When did they get up?

a Stamattina, io _____ alle sei (masc.).
b Il panettiere _____ alle quattro.
c Sua moglie _____ alle quattro e mezza.
d Berto _____ alle sette e mezza.
e Patrizio e Mariella _____ alle sette meno un quarto.
f Signora Cecilia, a che ora _____? (Lei)
g Noi _____ alle sei (masc.).
h I signori Pirelli _____ alle nove.
i Lucia e Carla, _____ alle nove e mezza, non è vero? (voi)
j A che ora _____ tu questa mattina, Paolo?

Here are some more reflexive verbs. You probably know most of them already.

Infinitive	Meaning	Present tense	Perfect tense
addormentarsi	to fall asleep	mi addormento	mi sono addormentato/a
annoiarsi	to get bored	mi annoio	mi sono annoiato/a
arrabbiarsi	to get angry	mi arrabbio	mi sono arrabbiato/a
divertirsi	to enjoy oneself	mi diverto	mi sono divertito/a
farsi la barba	to shave	mi faccio la barba	mi sono fatto la barba
lavarsi	to wash	mi lavo	mi sono lavato/a
pettinarsi	to comb one's hair	mi pettino	mi sono pettinato/a
preoccuparsi	to get worried	mi preoccupo	mi sono preoccupato/a
prepararsi	to get ready	mi preparo	mi sono preparato/a
ricordarsi	to remember	mi ricordo	mi sono ricordato/a
riposarsi	to rest	mi riposo	mi sono riposato/a
sbagliarsi	to make a mistake	mi sbaglio	mi sono sbagliato/a
sedersi	to sit down	mi siedo	mi sono seduto/a
smarrirsi	to get lost	mi smarrisco	mi sono smarrito/a
svegliarsi	to wake up	mi sveglio	mi sono svegliato/a
vestirsi	to get dressed	mi vesto	mi sono vestito/a

Checklist: the perfect tense

You use the perfect tense to talk about something which has happened at a specific time in the past.

Most verbs form the perfect tense with *avere* and the past participle of the verb: *ho mangiato.*

avere: ho, hai, ha, abbiamo, avete, hanno

Some verbs use *essere* instead: *sono arrivato;* with these, the past participle agrees with the subject.

essere: sono, sei, è, siamo, siete, sono

1.4.4 The imperfect tense: when to use it

▶▶ **If you know when to use the imperfect tense, go to 1.4.5.**

You use the imperfect tense to:

• describe what something was like in the past:

When I was small, we lived in Scotland.	Quando ero piccolo, abitavamo in Scozia.
The house was old.	La casa era vecchia.
It rained every day.	Pioveva ogni giorno.

• say what someone or something used to do:

I used to walk to school.	Andavo a scuola a piedi.
We used to look for wood for the fire.	Cercavamo legna per il fuoco.
My father used to go fishing.	Mio padre andava a pesca.

• describe an interrupted action (say what someone/ something was doing when something else happened):

| I was watching (imperfect) television when the phone rang (perfect). | Guardavo la tivù quando ha suonato il telefono. |

 If you use 'was' or 'were' or 'used to' in English, you need to use the imperfect to say the same thing in Italian.

 The imperfect is usually the tense to use for describing the weather in the past: *faceva freddo*, 'it was cold'; *pioveva*, 'it was raining'

1.4.5 How to form the imperfect tense

▶▶ **If you know how to form the imperfect tense go on to 1.4.6.**

To form the imperfect, you need to know the infinitive stem e.g. *parlare* > *parl-* and add the endings for *-are*, *-ere* and *-ire* verbs as appropriate. This makes it just about the easiest tense in Italian, with very few irregular verbs! Here are the regular forms:

Person	*-are* verb endings	*-ere* verb endings	*-ire* verb endings
io	-avo	-evo	-ivo
tu	-avi	-evi	-ivi
lui/lei/Lei	-ava	-eva	-iva
noi	-avamo	-evamo	-ivamo
voi	-avate	-evate	-ivate
loro/Loro	-avano	-evano	-ivano

You can see that the imperfect endings start with the vowel of the infinitive ending.

A Regular verbs

Here are complete examples of regular verbs; note that *-isc-* verbs are like all other *-ire* verbs here:

parlare	vendere	partire	finire
parlavo	vendevo	partivo	finivo
parlavi	vendevi	partivi	finivi
parlava	vendeva	partiva	finiva
parlavamo	vendevamo	partivamo	finivamo
parlavate	vendevate	partivate	finivate
parlavano	vendevano	partivano	finivano

XII *Cosa facevano?* What were they doing when the lights went out?

a Mio marito _____ davanti alla televisione. (dormire)
b Carlo _____ la televisione. (guardare)
c Chiara _____ una rivista. (leggere)
d Io _____ con la mia vicina. (chiacchierare)
e (Noi) _____ del nuovo presidente. (parlare)
f Sara si _____ la doccia. (fare)
g Francesco _____ alla sua ragazza. (telefonare)
h Andrea e la sua amica _____ le loro moto in garage. (riparare)
i Nicola e Alessandro _____ a biliardo. (giocare)

B Irregular verbs

Only a handful of verbs are irregular in the imperfect tense, but note that the endings are the same as those of regular verbs. Here are the most useful ones.

essere	bere	dire	fare
ero	bevevo	dicevo	facevo
eri	bevevi	dicevi	facevi
era	beveva	diceva	faceva
eravamo	bevevamo	dicevamo	facevamo
eravate	bevevate	dicevate	facevate
erano	bevevano	dicevano	facevano

XIII Give the correct form of the verb.

a She was quite small. _____ abbastanza piccola.
b They used to do a lot of sport. _____ molto sport.
c We were young. _____ giovani.
d You were a clever boy. _____ un ragazzo intelligente.

e I used to drink English beer. _____ birra inglese.
f You used to say that you were Tu _____ che morivi dalla voglia
dying to see me. di vedermi.

XIV Give the correct form of the imperfect of the verb in brackets.

a (Io) _____ alla fermata dell'autobus. (aspettare)
b (Tu) _____ Ligabue sul tuo walkman. (ascoltare)
c (Noi) _____ in città. (andare)
d Patrizio _____ il giornale. (leggere)
e (Lei) _____ il suo ragazzo. (aspettare)
f Mario _____ di casa. (uscire)
g I suoi genitori _____ in campagna. (stare)
h Silvia _____ footing. (fare)
i Voi _____ la televisione. (guardare)
j Mio padre _____ un aperitivo. (bere)

XV Complete the sentences to describe the weather by adding the correct form of the imperfect of the verb in brackets.

a _____ bel tempo. (fare)
b _____ (nevicare)
c C' _____ il sole. (essere)
d _____ vento. (tirare)
e _____ a catinelle. (piovere)
f _____ (tuonare)
g La nebbia _____ (dissolversi)
h _____ caldo. (fare)
i C' _____ un temporale. (essere)
j Il mare _____ molto mosso. (essere)

C Reflexive verbs in the imperfect

Reflexive verbs behave the same way in the imperfect tense as in the present, with the reflexive pronoun before the appropriate part of the verb, so they present no problems.

XVI In the old days ...

a Quando il mio bisnonno _____ piccolo, _____ in campagna. (essere, abitare)
b Le case _____ fatte di pietra. (essere)
c C' _____ meno di venti abitanti nel suo paese. (essere)
d Si _____ l'uva. (coltivare)
e I bambini _____ nella vigna. (lavorare)
f _____ l'uva. (raccogliere)
g I suoi genitori _____ il vino. (fare)
h Non c' _____ l'elettricità. (essere)
i Sua madre _____ in un fuoco di legna. (cucinare)
j Il mio bisnonno _____ andare a scuola a piedi. (dovere)
k Per andare a scuola, ci _____ un'ora. (volere)

Checklist: the imperfect tense

The imperfect tense is easy as it is always formed in the same way.

Take the infinitive of the verb, remove the *-are/ere/ire* and add the new endings.

The endings are the same for all verbs, and there are just a few irregular verbs. The endings:

for *-are* verbs are: *-avo, -avi, -ava, -avamo, -avate, -avano;*
for *-ere* verbs: *-evo, -evi, -eva, -evamo, -evate, -evano;*
and for *-ire* verbs: *-ivo, -ivi, -iva, -ivamo, -ivate, -ivano.*

You are most likely to need to use the imperfect tense when talking about yourself: *facevo ..., ero ..., avevo ...*

... or about the weather: *faceva ..., c'era ...,* etc.

1.4.6 Perfect or imperfect?

Remember to use the imperfect tense for the action that was ongoing, and the perfect tense for the action that 'interrupted' it.

XVII You need to use both the imperfect and the perfect in these sentences. Fill in the verbs in the appropriate tense, then translate the sentences.

a I suoi genitori _____ (abitare) a Livorno quando Nadia _____ (nascere).

b Quando lei _____ (essere) piccola, la sua famiglia _____ (andare) in Svizzera.

c Nadia _____ (avere) cinque anni quando suo fratello _____ (nascere).

d Giuseppe _____ (avere) un incidente quando _____ (avere) dieci anni.

e _____ (attraversare) la strada quando un'auto non _____ (fermarsi) al semaforo.

f Nadia _____ (vedere) l'incidente mentre _____ (aspettare) l'autobus.

g Lei _____ (avere) diciannove anni quando _____ (dare) l'esame di maturità.

h Nadia _____ (studiare) biologia quando _____ (decidere) di abbandonare i suoi studi.

i _____ (fare) un corso di informatica quando _____ (vedere) l'annuncio della MegaSA.

j Nadia _____ (lavorare) per questa ditta quando _____ (conoscere) il suo futuro marito.

k Lei _____ (essere) direttrice del personale quando lui _____ (fare) domanda d'impiego.

l _____ (fare) bel tempo quando Nadia e Giuseppe _____ (sposarsi).

1.4.7 The past definite tense: *il passato remoto*

 If you know about the past definite tense, go on to 1.4.8.

The past definite tense in Italian is just like the English past simple tense, consisting of just one word. However, you will only come across it occasionally: this is because it is not used in spoken form over most of Italy, the perfect tense being used instead. It is, however, commonly used for narrative in formal writing, for example in novels and historical writing. Here, we will just give you enough information to enable you to recognise it; for more information, consult *Azione Grammatica* (Hodder and Stoughton).

This tense is always used to describe a single, completed action in the past. The past definite tense is therefore used for narrative and reports of past events, only being used for recent everyday events in spoken Italian in southern Italy.

In Italian, most verbs form the past definite on a stem based on the infinitive minus *-are/ere/ire*. These examples could be expressed in the perfect tense if they concern recent actions, but are more likely to be in the past definite in written Italian.

Andai al bar e chiesi una birra.	I went to the bar and I ordered a beer.
Perdesti un coltello e rompesti una tazza.	You lost a knife and broke a cup.
Andò in città e fece la spesa.	S/he went to town and did some shopping.
Andammo alla stazione e prendemmo il treno delle sei.	We went to the station and got the 6 o'clock train.
Dimenticaste le chiavi e abbandonaste l'auto.	You forgot the keys and abandoned the car.
Andarono al mercato e comprarono delle pere.	They went to the market and bought pears.

Here are the past definite forms of regular *-are*, *-ere* and *-ire* verbs; note that *-ere* verbs have two possible forms for the *io*, *lui/lei* and *loro* forms:

-are: parlare	*-ere: vendere*	*-ire: partire*
parlai	vendei (vendetti)	partii
parlasti	vendesti	partisti
parlò	vendé (vendette)	partì
parlammo	vendemmo	partimmo
parlaste	vendeste	partiste
parlarono	venderono (vendettero)	partirono

There are many irregular verbs in the past definite tense; since this tense is not one you are likely to need, we will simply give you a selection of useful irregular verbs so that you can recognise the endings and how the stems of irregular verbs change from one form to another. With all but *essere*, there are identifiable patterns.

essere	*avere*	*chiudere*	*dire*	*fare*	*leggere*
fui	ebbi	chiusi	dissi	feci	lessi
fosti	avesti	chiudesti	dicesti	facesti	leggesti
fu	ebbe	chiuse	disse	fece	lesse
fummo	avemmo	chiudemmo	dicemmo	facemmo	leggemmo
foste	aveste	chiudeste	diceste	faceste	leggeste
furono	ebbero	chiusero	dissero	fecero	lessero

mettere	*muovere*	*nascere*	*prendere*	*ridere*	*stare*
misi	mossi	nacqui	presi	risi	stetti
mettesti	movesti	nascesti	prendesti	ridesti	stesti
mise	mosse	nacque	prese	rise	stette
mettemmo	movemmo	nascemmo	prendemmo	ridemmo	stemmo
metteste	moveste	nasceste	prendeste	rideste	steste
misero	mossero	nacquero	presero	risero	stettero

Can you observe the following features?

1. All have two stems.
2. The stems for *tu, noi* and *voi* are usually closest to the infinitive stem.
3. The stems for *io, lui/lei* and *loro* are irregular and often end in -*s*- or -*ss*-.
4. For all verbs, the past definite endings are: *io* = -*i*, *tu* = -*sti*, *noi* = -*mmo*, *voi* = -*ste*, *loro* = *rono* or -*ero*; *lui/lei* always ends in -*o*, -*e*, -*i*, for regular verbs usually with an accent and -*e* for irregular verbs.

As always, many other verbs follow these models.

XVIII   Storytelling in the past definite: put in the correct form of the right verb from the list below, then translate the story.

> Molti anni fa, (noi) __1__ in Italia. __2__ due settimane al mare. __3__ un appartamento a Diamante. Mio marito __4__ windsurf; io __5__ il tempo prendendo il sole sulla spiaggia e leggendo.
> Mio fratello e sua moglie __6__ a stare un fine settimana con noi. Ci __7__ molto. La sera __8__ in un ristorante e poi __9__ fino alle tre di notte. Il giorno dopo, tutti __10__ il windsurf. E voi, dove __11__ e cosa __12__ lì?

> affittare, ballare, cenare, divertirsi, fare (x 3), andare (x 2), passare, stare, venire

Checklist: the past definite tense

You use the past definite tense to talk about a single, completed action which happened at a specific time in the past.

Almost all verbs have regular endings, but there are many irregular verbs.

The endings for *-are* verbs are: *-ai, -asti, -ò, -ammo, -aste, -arono.*

The endings for *-ere* verbs are: *-ei/etti, -esti, -é/-ette, -emmo, -este, -erono/-ettero.*

The endings for *-ire* verbs are: *-ii, -isti, -ì, -immo, -iste, -irono.*

1.4.8 ▶Fast track: the past tenses

There are different ways of saying what has happened in the past

A The perfect tense

This is used to describe an action in the past which has been completed recently.

 The perfect tense is used whenever it is used in English, and also instead of the simple one-word past tense form, i.e. for both 'I have spoken' and 'I spoke'.

The perfect tense is made up of an auxiliary or 'helper' verb and the past participles, as in English: *avere* for most verbs – 'I have eaten' *ho mangiato* – and *essere* for some verbs, including all reflexives: 'we have arrived' *siamo arrivati*. Note that past participles with *essere* verbs always have to agree with the subject, and participles with *avere* verbs sometimes have to agree with a preceding direct object.

B The imperfect tense

The imperfect is used to talk about an ongoing or habitual action in the past.

If you can use 'was/were' or 'used to' in English you use the imperfect tense in Italian.

It is formed by adding to the infinitive stem the endings:
-avo, -avi, -ava, -avamo, -avate, -avano for *-are* verbs;
-evo, -evi, eva, -evamo, -evate, -evano for *-ere* verbs;
and *-ivo, -ivi, -iva, -ivamo, -ivate, -ivano* for *-ire* verbs.

C The past definite tense

C The past definite tense

This is used to describe a single, completed action in the distant past. It is often used where we might expect the perfect tense, but usually only in formal written reports.

To a stem based on the infinitive add:

for -are verbs: -ai, -asti, -ò, -ammo, -aste, -arono
for -ere verbs: -ei/-etti, -esti, -é/-ette, -emmo, -este, -erono/-ettero
for -ire verbs: -ii, -isti, -ì, -immo, -iste, -irono

There are many irregular verbs in this tense.

1.5 The future tense and the conditional

A The future: *il futuro*

You use the future tense, *il futuro*, to talk about something that is going to happen, something you want to do or are going to do in the future. In Italian, just as in English, there are two ways of saying what is going to happen. Note also that the present tense is often used to express an event which will happen in the near future (see section 1.2).

The future tense translates the English 'will' and can imply intention as well as future action, e.g. 'He will go' – 'I will make sure he does!'

guarderò	I will watch
andrà	he will go
ascolteranno	they will listen

B The conditional: *il condizionale*

This is not strictly considered a future tense but it talks about the future: what you would do if ...

It translates 'would/should/could' in English. 'I would like to go if ...', talking about something you would like to do in the future.

I would like to go to Rome.
We really should/ought to go.
Could we go tomorrow?

It is also used as a more polite way of stating or asking for something:

'I would like to leave now': *Mi piacerebbe andare via subito.*

1.5.1 The future tense: 'I will ...'

▶▶ **If you know about the future tense go on to 1.5.2.**

This is the 'proper' future tense, sometimes called the future simple because it consists of just one word. It translates the English 'will' and is used to talk about events which will take place in the future.

comprerò	I will buy
andrà	he will go
ascolteranno	they will listen

A Regular verbs

Fortunately almost all verbs are regular. The *futuro* is made by adding these endings to a stem based on the infinitive: *-ò, -ai, -à, -emo, -ete, -anno. -are* and *-ere* verbs use the infinitive stem adding *-er-*, and *-ire* verbs add *-ir* before the future tense ending. A few verbs have a slighly modified future stem.

 Notice the endings are very similar to those of the present tense of the verb *avere* except for the *noi* and the *voi* forms.

This may help you to remember them:

-are verbs	*-ere* verbs	*-ire* verbs
parlerò	prenderò	partirò
parlerai	prenderai	partirai
parlerà	prenderà	partirà
parleremo	prenderemo	partiremo
parlerete	prenderete	partirete
parleranno	prenderanno	partiranno

I Give the correct future tense of the verbs in brackets.

a noi _____ (guardare)
b tu _____ (preparare)
c voi _____ (mettere)
d loro _____ (mangiare)
e Lei _____ (permettere)
f lui _____ (scrivere)
g loro _____ (arrivare)
h noi _____ (entrare)
i io _____ (partire)
j loro _____ (salire)

II *Cosa porteranno?* What are they going to wear for the *festa?*

a Io _____ i vestiti tradizionali della regione.
b Voi _____ una gonna rossa e una camicetta bianca.

c Il mio amico _____ il suo completo nero e una camicia bianca.
d Nicola _____ i suoi jeans e una maglietta, come sempre.
e Le mie amiche _____ il loro vestito nazionale.
f I miei amici _____ dei pantaloni neri e una camicia azzurra.
g Noi _____ dei calzettoni bianchi e delle scarpe nere.
h E Lei, che _____?
i Che _____ tu?

B   Irregular verbs

Some of the most common verbs are irregular in the future
tense.

 Look for patterns to help you remember them and choose the four
that you think you are most likely to need, and learn the *io* form.

Here are the most useful irregular future verbs starting with
essere, which is completely irregular; with the others the
stem is only slightly irregular, losing the vowel of the
infinitive ending; but the endings are the same for all verbs.

essere

sarò
sarai
sarà
saremo
sarete
saranno

Infinitive	Future
andare	andrò
avere	avrò
cadere	cadrò
dovere	dovrò
potere	potrò
sapere	saprò
vedere	vedrò
vivere	vivrò

The following verbs have future stems ending in *-rr-*:

Infinitive	Future
bere	berrò
morire	morrò
parere	parrò
rimanere	rimarrò

Infinitive	Future
tenere	terrò
valere	varrò
venire	verrò
volere	vorrò

Note also the following:

Infinitive	Future
dare	darò
fare	farò
stare	starò
cominciare	comincerò
mangiare	mangerò
cercare	cercherò
pagare	pagherò

As you can see, *dare, fare, stare* keep the *-a-* of their infinitives, *cominciare* and *mangiare* lose the *-i*, unnecessary before the *-e-*, and *cercare* and *mangiare* need *-h-* to keep the hard *-c-* or *-g-* sound before the *-e-*.

Note that, as always, any compounds based on the verbs above have the same irregularity in the future tense; in the case of the last group, verbs with similar spellings have the same changes.

Useful expressions: *te lo dirò più tardi*, 'I'll tell you later'; *sarà necessario*, 'it will be necessary'.

III For more practice give the correct form of the verb in brackets.

a io _____ (avere)
b voi _____ (venire)
c tu _____ (fare)
d noi _____ (avere)
e lui _____ (salire)
f lei _____ (sapere)
g Loro _____ (volere)
h noi _____ (dire)
i voi _____ (mettere)
j loro _____ (potere)
k Lei _____ (tenere)
l io _____ (venire)

IV Write in the correct form of the verb in brackets:

    a L'anno prossimo, io _____ vent'anni. (avere)
    b In questo momento, studio in Italia, ma l'anno prossimo io _____ in Inghilterra. (andare)
    c Io _____ un corso d'inglese a Oxford. (fare)
    d (Io) ti _____ il mio nuovo indirizzo. (mandare)
    e Tu _____ a trovarmi a Oxford, vero? (venire)
    f Poi, noi _____ insieme a Londra. (andare)
    g _____ anche fare un viaggio in Scozia, ma _____ necessario andare in auto perché andare con il treno _____ troppo! (potere, essere, costare)
    h Quando _____ il mio corso, io _____ in Italia, e _____ per mio padre nel suo ufficio. (finire, tornare, lavorare).

V What are these people going to do? Complete the sentences by adding the correct form of the verb *andare*.

    a Io _____ alla spiaggia a fare del windsurf.
    b Tu _____ in montagna a fare deltaplano.
    c Mario _____ al fiume a fare del rafting.
    d Lei _____ al mare a fare surf.
    e Noi _____ al salone dell'automobile per comprare un'auto con quattro ruote motrici.
    f Voi _____ sulle Alpi per fare lo sci.
    g Natalia e Sergio _____ sulle Alpi a fare snowboard.
    h Loro _____ in montagna a fare alpinismo?
    i Patrizio e Benedetto _____ sugli Apennini a fare speleologia.
    j Io _____ a casa.

VI *Il compleanno di Davide.* What are they going to do for Davide's birthday? Add the missing part of the future tense verb.

    a I suoi colleghi organizzer _____ una festa.
    b Tommaso far _____ una torta.
    c Sabrina spedir _____ gli inviti.
    d Isabella e Silvia preparer _____ qualcosa da mangiare.
    e Sergio comprer _____ cinque bottiglie di Asti Spumante.
    f Il suo padrone gli offrir _____ un regalo.
    g Raffaele decorer _____ la casa.
    h Noi aiuter _____ Raffaele.
    i Silvia cercher _____ i bicchieri.
    j Voi canter _____ «Tanti auguri a te!».

VII Bianca and Riccardo and their children are going skiing in the Swiss Alps. Before they leave they go over the travel arrangements with the travel agent. Add the correct form of the verb in brackets; most need to be in the *voi* form; watch out for the others.

a Quando _____ (noi)? (partire)
b (Voi) _____ il volo di Alitalia delle 14:50. (prendere)
c Un pullman vi _____ al vostro arrivo e vi _____ all'albergo.
(aspettare/portare)
d Voi tutti _____ sciare. (potere)
e A mezzogiorno, (voi) _____ all'albergo o in un ristorante, come
_____ (pranzare/volere)
f La sera (voi) _____ uscire. (potere)
g Siccome _____ freddo, (voi) _____ portare sempre vestiti adatti.
(fare/dovere)

1.5.2 The conditional: 'I would ...'

▶▶ **If you don't want to practise the conditional go to
1.5.4, as you might need to recognise it when you
hear it.**

 You probably already know the expressions *vorrei* and *mi
piacerebbe* for 'I would like', both good examples of the conditional.

The conditional is used to translate 'would', 'could' and
'should' in English. It is called the conditional because you
use it when you are making a condition: 'I would go if you
paid me!' But it is also used to be more polite: 'I would like
a box of chocolates'.

1.5.3 How to form the conditional

It is easy to learn as it uses the same stem as the future tense
+ a special set of endings which are the same for all verbs.

A Regular verbs

-are verbs	*-ere* verbs	*-ire* verbs
parlerei	venderei	partirei
parleresti	venderesti	partiresti
parlerebbe	venderebbe	partirebbe
parleremmo	venderemmo	partiremmo
parlereste	vendereste	partireste
parlerebbero	venderebbero	partirebbero

VIII How would you say the following?

I would ...

a eat (mangiare)
b drink (bere)
c sleep (dormire)

d speak (parlare)
e live (vivere)
f buy (comprare)
g ask (chiedere)
h listen (ascoltare)
i watch (guardare)

IX Add the right part of *giocare* to the following. Remember the spelling change.

a I would play tennis.   Io _____ a tennis.
b My friend would play too.   La mia amica _____ anche lei.
c Her friends would play too.   Anche i suoi amici _____ .
d We wouldn't play.   Noi non _____ .
e You would play volleyball.   Voi _____ a pallavolo.

X Add the right part of *preferire* to these sentences.

a I would prefer to go to the beach.   Io _____ andare alla spiaggia.
b My boyfriend would prefer to go windsurfing.   Il mio ragazzo _____ fare windsurf.
c My girlfriends would prefer to go to town.   Le mie amiche _____ andare al paese.
d We would prefer to dine in a restaurant.   Noi _____ cenare in un ristorante.
e What would you prefer to do?   Cosa _____ fare voi?

XI *Piacere* and a few other verbs are 'back-to-front' verbs. Add the right part of each one, and the correct pronoun (see sections 1.2.2 and 1.9.6).

a I would like to go out.   _____ uscire. (piacere)
b Gino would like to stay in.   A Gino _____ rimanere a casa. (piacere)
c Patrizia is interested in going to the cinema.   A Patrizia _____ andare al cinema. (interessare)
d My parents would be interested in going to Austria.   Ai miei genitori _____ andare in Austria. (interessare)
e Would you like some books, Pino?   _____ dei libri, Pino? (piacere)
f What would you like to do, boys and girls?   Cosa _____ fare, ragazzi? (piacere)
g What would you like to do, Signor Piaggio?   Che _____ fare, Signor Piaggio? (piacere)
h Would you be interested in theatre tickets, Signori?   Vi _____ dei biglietti del teatro, Signori? (interessare)

B Irregular verbs

In the conditional, irregular verbs use the same stem as for the future, but with conditional endings. As a reminder, here they are, starting with the full set of forms for *essere*.

essere
sarei
saresti
sarebbe
saremmo
sareste
sarebbero

Verbs with shortened infinitve stems:

Infinitive	Future
andare	andrei
avere	avrei
cadere	cadrei
dovere	dovrei
potere	potrei
sapere	saprei
vedere	vedrei
vivere	vivrei

Verbs with -*rr*- stem:

Infinitive	Future
bere	berrei
morire	morrei
parere	parrei
rimanere	rimarrei
tenere	terrei
valere	varrei
venire	verrei
volere	vorrei

Verbs with modified stem spellings:

Infinitive	Future
dare	darei
fare	farei
stare	starei
cominciare	comincerei
mangiare	mangerei
cercare	cercherei
pagare	pagherei

XII Talking about yourself: how would you say the following?

a I would make something to eat.

Io _____ da mangiare. (preparare)

b I would leave town.

_____ dalla città. (uscire)

c I would have a friend.

_____ un amico. (avere)

d I would tell my friends.

Lo _____ ai miei amici. (dire)

e I would come to Italy.

_____ in Italia. (venire)

f I could windsurf.

_____ fare windsurf. (potere)

g I would put on a coat.

Mi _____ il cappotto. (mettere)

h I would know the answer.

_____ la risposta. (sapere)

i I would want to go out.

Io _____ uscire. (volere)

j I would have written to him.

Io gli _____ scritto. (avere)

XIII What could they do? Fill in the correct form of *potere*.

a Nadia could go home.

Nadia _____ tornare a casa.

b We could go to the cinema.

Noi _____ andare al cinema.

c We could go to the sports centre.

_____ andare al centro sportivo.

d I could do karate.

Io _____ fare karate.

e You could play volleyball.

Tu _____ giocare a pallavolo.

f Concetta could go riding.

Concetta _____ andare a cavallo.

g The children could go swimming.

I bambini _____ andare in piscina.

h We could meet afterwards.

_____ incontrarci dopo.

i We could go to the bar.

_____ andare al bar.

j We could go back to my house.

_____ tornare a casa mia.

1.5.4 ▶Fast track: the future and conditional

To say what you are going to do or what is going to happen, use the future tense *il futuro* which is made up from a stem based on the infinitive with endings: *-ò, -ai, -à, -emo, -ete, -anno.*

These are the most commonly used irregular verbs in the future. It is useful to be able to recognise which verb they come from.

andare	andrò
avere	avrò
dovere	dovrò
essere	sarò
fare	farò
pagare	pagherò
potere	potrò
sapere	saprò
stare	starò

vedere	vedrò
venire	verrò
vivere	vivrò
volere	vorrò

The conditional translates 'would', e.g. 'I would go', 'I would like'.

You probably already know *vorrei* and *mi piacerebbe* ('I would like'), so you already know a couple of the endings.

The most useful conditionals are:

mi piacerebbe	I would like
vorrei	I would love
preferirei	I would prefer
potremmo	we could
dovremmo	we should, ought to
sarebbe	it would be

1.6 The subjunctive

▶▶ **If you are not ready for the subjunctive yet go on to section 1.8.**

The subjunctive is not used much in English any more (only in expressions such as 'If I were you' ...), but it has to be used in many expressions in Italian. You are not likely to need to use those expressions yourself very often other than those forms used for imperatives which you have already met (see 1.3.3), but it is useful to be able to recognise them when you hear them and you may need to know which verb is being used. Choose one or two of the expressions to learn by heart and then use them as a model.

If you want to know more about the subjunctive go to *Azione Grammatica* (Hodder and Stoughton).

The subjunctive is very often preceded by the word *che*. BUT this does not mean that *che* is always followed by the subjunctive!

In Italian, the subjunctive is used after verbs which express a wish or desire:

Voglio che vada lui.	I want him to go.
Spero che lei venga.	I hope that she will come.

... or a requirement (after *bisogna che/è necessario che*, ('it is necessary that'):

Bisogna che lui sappia guidare.   He must be able to drive.

or a doubt or uncertainty:

Non credo che abbia soldi.   I don't think (that) he has any money

È possibile che i bambini siano   It is possible that the children
stanchi.   are tired.

and after certain fixed expressions such as:

'in order that', *affinché/in modo che*.

affinchè lui arrivi in tempo   in order that he arrives on time

'although', *benché*.

benché lei parta alle 6:00   although she leaves at 6 o'clock

'before', *prima che*.

prima che lui compri il suo biglietto   before he buys his ticket

'until', *finché non*:

finché non arrivi alla stazione   until he arrives at the station

 If in doubt, look at a good dictionary: they will often give examples of expressions using these and other constructions, from which you can see when the subjunctive is necessary.

1.6.1 How to form the subjunctive

Put simply, the subjunctive is formed with the same stem as the present tense, and by and large follows the same patterns of spelling variation from one person form to another.

For *-are* verbs, the subjunctive endings are:

-i, -i, -i, -iamo, -iate, -ino

and for *-ere* and *-ire* verbs, the subjunctive endings are:

-a, -a, -a, -iamo, -iate, -ano

Can you spot the following features?

- *-are* verbs have endings mostly with a dominant *-i-*, not the *-a-* you would expect.
- *-ere* and *-ire* verbs have endings mostly with a dominant *-a-* instead of *-i-*.

- Forms for *io, tu, lui, lei* and *Lei* are all the same.
- The *noi* forms are the same as for the 'normal' present (the indicative).

You will recognise most of these forms from the imperative use of the subjunctive (see 1.3.3). As you can see, the *io* form does not end in *-o* as in the normal present tense (indicative), but is the same as the second and third person singular. So *io, tu, lui, lei, Lei* are used in front of the verb to clarify who is the person doing the action

There are obvious patterns: once you know one form, the others follow very predictably and easily.

A   Regular verbs

io form	parlare	io form	vendere	io form	partire	io form	preferire
parlo	parli	vendo	venda	parto	parta	preferisco	preferisca
	parli		venda		parta		preferisca
	parli		venda		parta		preferisca
	parliamo		vendiamo		partiamo		preferiamo
	parliate		vendiate		partiate		preferiate
	parlino		vendano		partano		preferiscano

Note that *preferire* and similar verbs use the long *-isc-* form for the same persons as in the normal present tense.

B   Spelling-change verbs

Spelling-change verbs follow very obvious rules, as in the present tense:

c+h before -i-	g+h before -i-	Removal of -i-
cercare	pagare	mangiare
cerchi	paghi	mangi
cerchi	paghi	mangi
cerchi	paghi	mangi
cerchiamo	paghiamo	mangiamo
cerchiate	paghiate	mangiate
cerchino	paghino	mangino

C   Irregular verbs

The most useful irregular verbs are in any case ones which will be familiar to you because you see and hear them a lot as instructions in public places. For other forms of these verbs in the subjunctive, check the verb tables at the end of this book.

93

Verbs

Infinitive	Present *io* form	Subjunctive
andare	vado	vada
avere	ho	abbia
bere	bevo	beva
dare	do	dia
dire	dico	dica
dovere	devo	deva (debba)
essere	sono	sia
fare	faccio	faccia
piacere	piaccio	piaccia
potere	posso	possa
salire	salgo	salga
sapere	so	sappia
sedere	siedo	sieda
stare	sto	stia
tenere	tengo	tenga
uscire	esco	esca
venire	vengo	venga
volere	voglio	voglia

1.6.2 Expressions which take the subjunctive

These expressions are always followed by the subjunctive, and they are only examples.

Choose two to memorise as a pattern.

Expressions of necessity

È necessario che me ne vada.	I have to go.
Bisogna che lei lo sappia.	She has to know.

Futurity and purpose

Prenderò il treno affinchè il viaggio sia comodo.	I'll take the train so that the journey will be comfortable.
La chiameremo perché sappia la notizia.	We'll call her to tell her the news.

Wishes, influence or preferences

Voglio che lui arrivi in tempo.	I want him to be on time.
Preferisce che io vada lì.	He prefers me to go (there).

Possibility

È possibile che lui possa venire.	It is possible that he can come.
È impossibile che lui arrivi in ritardo.	It is not possible for him to be late.

Doubt and disbelief

Non credo che lui sia malato.	I don't believe that he is ill.
Penso che lei venga.	I think she will come.

Emotion and judgement

Mi dispiace che lui sia stato ferito.	I am sorry that he has been hurt.
È un peccato che tu non possa venire.	It's a pity that you can't come.

Conjunctions such as *benché*, 'although' and *sebbene*, 'even if'

Benché Lei sia malato, deve presentarsi in tribunale.	Although you are ill, you have to go to court.

 Essentially, the subjunctive is used whenever the statement is looking forward, or refers to an unfulfilled or hypothetical action. Ask yourself 'did it happen/is it happening/will it happen?' If the answer is 'no', or 'not yet', you probably need the subjunctive.

Note that the subjunctive forms for *Lei* and *Loro* are used as imperative forms.

1.6.3 Recognising the subjunctive

Even if you do not feel ready to use the subjunctive yet, it is useful to be able to recognise it when you hear it.

I Which verb is being used? Read the sentence and work out the infinitive of the word in italics.

a	È necessario che *venga*.	He must come.
b	Non penso che *prenda* l'autobus.	I don't believe he'll come by bus.
c	Sono contento che *faccia* bel tempo oggi.	I'm pleased that it's fine today.
d	Spero che vi *sentiate* benvenuti!	I hope you feel welcome!
e	È possibile che *siano* malati.	It's possible that they are ill.
f	Sebbene *abbia* l'auto, andrà sempre a piedi.	Even if she has a car, she will always go on foot.
g	Bisogna che lo *sappia* lei.	She will have to know.
h	È impossibile che si *possa* finire in tempo.	It's impossible for it to be completed in time.
i	Dubito che *abbiano* un'auto nuova.	I don't think (doubt) they have a new car.
j	Mi dispiace molto che *vogliate* partire.	I am very sorry that you want to go.

1.6.4 ▶Fast track: the subjunctive

The subjunctive is used after certain verbs and expressions. It usually conveys a feeling of negativity, uncertainty, doubt or indecision: 'I don't want', 'I am not sure that', 'It is possible that', etc.

It is usually preceded by a conjunction or another verb and *che*, 'that':

I hope/wish/doubt that ...

i.e. it is usually the second verb in the sentence.

The subjunctive of most verbs is made from a stem based on the infinitive. Remove the infinitive ending and then add these endings for *-are* verbs: *-i, -i, -i, -iamo, -iate, -ino* and these for *-ere* and *-ire* verbs: *-a, -a, -a, -iamo, -iate, -ano*.

Although many of the most commonly used verbs are irregular, some of the subjunctive forms are familiar as commands (imperative forms) in public notices and instructions. You don't need to learn them but it is useful to be able to recognise which verb they come from:

andare – vada
avere – abbia
dire – dica
essere – sia
fare – faccia
prendere – prenda
sapere – sappia
sedere – sieda
venire – venga

You can try to avoid using the subjunctive

• by being positive and avoiding making negative statements!

• using *secondo me* or *a mio avviso* to express an opinion,

• using the infinitive instead of *che* + subjunctive where possible:

Bisogna che beviamo due litri d'acqua al giorno ('We have to drink two litres of water a day') becomes:

Dobbiamo bere 2 litri d'acqua al giorno.

Think of an easier way of saying it in English. Don't use two verbs joined by 'that' in one sentence. Split it up and make two sentences: 'I am sorry that he is ill',

Mi dispiace che sia malato.

È malato? Mi dispiace!

Choose two or three examples to memorise, and use them as a pattern.

Of course, since nothing is ever simple, the subjunctive has forms in other tenses too, but you will not come across them often. If you want to know more, then consult *Azione Grammatica*.

1.7 Other tenses

Just when you think you have learned all the tenses, you pick up a book or a newspaper and find that there are even more. Fortunately, you don't have to learn to use them to speak good Italian. If you want to know more about these other tenses go to *Azione Grammatica*.

Here, to give you a flavour, is one extra tense which you may find useful to be able to recognise: the pluperfect. This is formed in the same way as the perfect tense except that instead of the present tense of *avere* or *essere*, it uses the imperfect. Here are some examples:

Prima di uscire, avevo mangiato.	Before going out I had eaten.
Ho chiamato Luigi, ma era già partito.	I called Luigi, but he had already left.
Avevano lavorato molto.	They had worked hard.
Eravamo saliti alle due.	We had gone up at two o'clock.

As you can see, this tense takes a jump one step further back into the past, to a time when something had happened before the main time-frame. Here are examples of an *avere* verb and an *essere* verb in the pluperfect tense.

avere + studiato	Meaning	essere + arrivato	Meaning
avevo studiato	I (had) studied	ero arrivato/a	I (had) arrived
avevi studiato	you (had) studied	eri arrivato/a	you (had) arrived
aveva studiato	he/she (had) studied	era arrivato/a	he/she (had) arrived
avevamo studiato	we (had) studied	eravamo arrivati/e	we (had) arrived
avevate studiato	you (had) studied	eravate arrivati/e	you (had) arrived
avevano studiato	they (had) studied	erano arrivati/e	they (had) arrived

1.8 ▶Fast track: verbs

▶▶ **If you know when to use the different tenses etc., go on to 1.9.**

A Present

You use the present tense to talk about what is happening now:

Leggo.	I am reading.

and to express generalisations:

Non guardo molto la televisione.	I don't watch much television.

These are the question forms:

Leggi (tu) un giornale?	Do you read a daily paper?
Guardi (tu) ...?	Do you watch ...?

B Perfect

You use the perfect tense to talk about what has happened at a specific moment in the past.

Ho giocato a tennis.	I (have) played tennis.
Ho provato a farlo.	I (have) tried to do it.

These are the question forms:

Hai giocato (tu)?	Have you played?
Hai provato a farlo?	Did you try to do it?

C Imperfect

You use the imperfect tense to talk about what has happened in the past if:

- it was a habitual action:

Giocavo quando ero piccolo/a.	I used to play (when I was young).

- it was an ongoing and interrupted action:

Guardavo la televisione quando ho sentito un rumore.	I was watching television when I heard a noise.

These are the question forms.

Giocavi (tu) ...?	Did you use to play ...?
Guardavi (tu) la televisione quando ...?	Were you watching television when ...?

D Past definite

You use the past definite tense or *passato remoto* to write about what happened at a defined moment in the not-so-recent past.

Giocò a tennis.	He played tennis.
Arrivarono l'anno scorso.	They arrived last year.

E Future

The future tense is used to express intention of what you are going to do in the future.

Farò ordine nel mio ufficio domani.	I will tidy my office tomorrow.
Fra poco andremo in Messico.	Soon we will go to Mexico.

These are the question forms:

Che farai (tu)?	What will you do?
Quando partirai?	When will you go?

F Imperative

The imperative is used to give orders or instructions.

Va' a prendermi le pantofole!	Fetch me my slippers! (tu)
Chiuda la porta, per favore!	Shut the door, please! (Lei)
Venite a trovarmi presto.	Come to see me soon. (voi)
Mettano le loro valigie lì.	Put your suitcases there. (Loro)

G Interrogative

The interrogative is used to ask questions.

Hai ...?	Have you got a ...?
Hai visto ...?	Did you see ...?

H Conditional

The conditional is used to put things more politely:

Mi piacerebbe ...	I would like ...
Potrebbe aiutarmi?	Could you help me?

or to express conditions:

Io ti comprerei un regalo se avessi abbastanza soldi.	I would buy you a present if I had enough money.

I Subjunctive

The subjunctive is used after certain verbs and expressions. It is usually preceded by another verb and *che*, 'that'.

You can avoid having to use it yourself by keeping sentences simple.

Subjunctive verbs seem to have the 'wrong' endings: based on -*i*- for -*are* verbs, and based on -*a*- for -*ere* and -*ire* verbs.

Irregular verbs mostly sound familiar because they are often used for public notices and instructions. In any case, you can always tell which verb they come from, e.g.:

sia – essere
tenga – tenere
vada – andare
faccia – fare
sappia – sapere

Recognising a verb

- If a word that you don't know comes after a noun, the name of a person or after a pronoun (*io, tu, lui, lei, Lei, noi, voi, loro* or *Loro*), it is probably a verb.
- If it ends in -*are*, -*ere*, -*ire*, -*arsi*, -*ersi* or -*irsi*, it is an an infinitive.
- If it comes after a part of *avere* or *essere* and ends in -*to*, it is a past participle of a verb.
- If it ends in -*o*, -*i*, -*a*, -*e*, -*iamo*, -*ate*, -*ete*, -*ite*, -*ano* or -*ono*, it is probably a verb in the present tense.
- If it ends in -*avo*, -*avi*, -*ava*, -*avamo*, -*avate*, -*avano* or -*evo*, -*evi*, -*eva*, -*evamo*, -*evate*, -*evano* or -*ivo*, -*ivi*, -*iva*, -*ivamo*, -*ivate*, -*ivano* it is definitely a verb in the imperfect tense.
- If it ends in -*rò*, -*rai*, -*rà*, -*remo*, -*rete*, -*ranno*, it is definitely a verb in the future tense.
- If it ends in -*rei*, -*resti*, -*rebbe*, -*remmo*, -*reste*, -*rebbero*, it is definitely a verb in the conditional tense.
- If it ends in -*ai*, -*asti*, -*ò*, -*ammo*, -*aste*, -*arono*, or -*ei*, -*este*, -*é*, -*emmo*, -*este*, -*erono* or -*ii*, -*isti*, -*ì*, -*immo*, -*iste*, -*irono*, it is the past definite form of a verb.

1.9 Useful expressions using verbs

▶▶ **If you know all these go on to 1.9.12.**

A *Essere* and *stare*

Some everyday expressions using 'to be' in English do not use *essere* in Italian but *stare* instead. However, *essere* is the most used.

B 'There is/are': *c'è, ci sono*

The Italian expressions for 'there is/are' are *c'è* and *ci sono* respectively.

C 'To have': special uses of *avere*

Avere is used for a host of special expressions, and in a few where we would expect *essere*.

D 'To know'

There are two verbs for 'to know' in Italian – to know a person or thing, *conoscere*, and to know a fact, *sapere*.

E Impersonal verbs

These are expressions in which there is no particular subject; they include many common, everyday expressions such as time and weather.

F 'Back to front' verbs

Piacere, *interessare* and one or two others are used with the object liked, loved etc. as the subject.

G 'To take', 'to bring' and 'to look for/fetch/meet a person'

Prendere and *portare*

H 'To remember', and 'to forget'

Ricordarsi di, 'to remember' ('to remind yourself of') and *dimenticarsi*, 'to forget'

If you don't know them well, study the following sections.

1.9.1 *Essere* and *stare*

Some everyday expressions using 'to be' in English use *stare* rather than *essere* in Italian, though in fact *essere* is the most used. An easy way to decide which to use is to remember that:

essere comes from Latin *esse*, 'to be', so use *essere* for what is of the *essence*, *essential*, i.e. to say what something or somebody *is* or is *like*.

I am a teacher, I am English, I am old – Sono professore, sono inglese, sono vecchio

stare comes from Latin *stare*, 'to stand', so use *stare* for anything involving position, and in just a few cases state. It is used for saying *where* something or somebody is, or what *state* they are in.

sto qui – I am staying here; sta' zitto – be quiet!; stare fermo – to be still; stare seduto – to be seated; stare in piedi – to stand; come stai? – how are you?

There are many impersonal expressions consisting of *essere* plus an adjective, e.g.

è necessario – it is necessary
è vietato – it is forbidden

Note that instead of *essere*, *avere* is often used in expressions where we would use the verb 'to be' in English.

e.g. In Italian you don't say: 'I am 21' but 'I have 21 years', *Ho 21 anni.*

For more of these, see 1.9.3.

I Which verb would you use to translate the following?

 a He is a student.
 b They are at home.
 c We are Italian.
 d Stay still!
 e I am a Ferrari fan.

1.9.2 'There is/are': *c'è, ci sono*

The Italian impersonal expressions for 'there is/are' are very similar to English, and transfer easily into other tenses by using the appropriate form of *essere* in the tense required:

C'è molto da fare.	There is a lot to do.
C'è frutta?	Is there any fruit?
C'è una pera.	There is one pear ...
... e ci sono molte arance.	... and there are lots of oranges.
Non c'era pane.	There was no bread.
C'erano dei pasticcini.	There were some cakes.
Ci sarà qualcos'altro?	Will there be anything else?
Sì, ci saranno dei biscotti.	Yes, there will be some biscuits.
Ieri c'è stato un temporale.	Yesterday there was a storm.

II Describe the room you are in using *c'è* and *ci sono*.

1.9.3 'To have': special uses of *avere*

Avere is used in some expressions where 'have' is not used in English. First, a reminder of the verb *avere* in the present tense:

ho, hai, ha, abbiamo, avete, hanno

Here are the expressions which use *avere* in this way: note the abbreviated form *aver* which is often used for the infinitive in such expressions.

Expressing age: *avere ... anni,* 'to be ... years old':

Quanti anni hai?	How old are you?
Ho 21 anni.	I am 21.

Expressing heat and cold: *aver caldo/freddo*

Ho freddo.	I am cold.
Ha freddo Lei?	Are you cold?
Hanno molto freddo.	They are very cold.
Hai caldo?	Are you hot?
Lei ha caldo.	She is hot.
Avete caldo, non è vero?	You are hot, aren't you?

Expressing hunger and thirst: *aver fame/sete*, 'to be hungry/thirsty':

Ho fame.	I am hungry.
Hai sete?	Are you thirsty?
Ha sete anche lei.	She is thirsty too.
Avete fame?	Are you hungry?
Non abbiamo fame.	We are not hungry.
Non avete sete!	You are not thirsty!
Non hanno molta fame.	They are not very hungry.

Expressing fear: *aver paura (di)*, 'to be afraid (of)':

Ho paura di te!	I am afraid of you!
Abbiamo paura del fulmine.	We are afraid of the lightning.
I bambini hanno paura del tuono.	The children are afraid of the thunder.
Loro non hanno paura di niente.	They fear nothing.

Being right or wrong: *aver ragione*, 'to be right':

Hai ragione!	You are right!
Ho ragione, vedi?	I am right, as you can see!
Non avete ragione.	You are not right/you are wrong.
Non abbiamo ragione.	We are wrong.

Being in a hurry: *aver fretta*, 'to be in a hurry':

Ho fretta.	I am in a hurry.
Avete fretta?	Are you in a hurry?

Being sleepy: *aver sonno*, 'to be sleepy':

Ho molto sonno.	I am very sleepy
Hai sonno?	Are you feeling sleepy?

Being lucky or unlucky: *aver fortuna*, 'to be lucky':

Hai avuto fortuna!	You've been lucky!
Abbiamo molta fortuna, non è vero?	We are very lucky, aren't we?
Non hanno fortuna.	They are not lucky.
Lei non avrà molta fortuna.	You are not going to have much luck.

Checklist: expressions taking avere

avere ... anni	to be ... years old
aver paura di	to be afraid
aver freddo/caldo	to be cold/hot
aver fame/sete	to be hungry/thirsty
(non) aver ragione	to be right/wrong
aver fortuna	to be lucky
aver sonno	to be tired
aver fretta	to be in a hurry
aver mal di ...	to have a pain in the ...

III How would you say the following?

a We are right.
b You are wrong. (tu)
c I am hot.
d He is thirsty.
e They are hungry.
f We are cold.
g I am thirsty.
h You are very sleepy. (Lei)
i We are lucky.
j I am in a hurry.

And some more:

k They are wrong.
l I am very cold.
m They are hot.
n We are thirsty.
o I am afraid of spiders.
p Are you thirsty? (tu)
q Are you cold? (Lei)
r Are you hot? (voi)
s Are you hungry? (Loro)
t Are you right? (tu)
u You are wrong! (Lei)
v Are you afraid? (voi)
w I am not afraid.
x He is not afraid.
y We are not afraid.
z He is always right.

Being in pain: *aver male/far male*

As in English, there are two ways of saying that something hurts or that you have a ... ache.

aver mal di	to have a pain in the .../to have a bad/sore .../... hurts
ho mal di testa	I have a headache
ho mal di stomaco	I have a stomach ache
far male a	to have a ... ache
mi fa male il naso	My nose hurts
Ieri mi facevano male i piedi	Yesterday my feet ached

Parts of the body which might hurt:

Singular	Plural	Meaning
il braccio	le braccia*	arm(s)
il dente	i denti	tooth, teeth
il dito	le dita	finger(s)
la gamba	le gambe	leg(s)
la gola		throat
la mano	le mani	hand(s)
l'occhio	gli occhi	eye(s)
l'orecchio	gli orecchi/le orecchie	ear(s)
il piede	i piedi	foot, feet
la schiena		back
lo stomaco		stomach

* Note that braccio is masculine in the singular but feminine in the plural.

IV How would you say the following? Experience will tell you which expression to use, though in most cases either expression can be used.

a I have a headache.
b Have you got a toothache? (tu)
c Her foot hurts.
d My arms ache.
e His knee hurts.
f Have you got a headache? (Lei)
g She has earache.
h Do your eyes hurt? (voi)
i Does your back hurt? (Loro)
j He has backache.

1.9.4 'To know': *sapere* or *conoscere*?

There are two verbs for 'to know' in Italian – *sapere* for 'to know a fact' or 'to be able to', and *conoscere* for 'to know a person or thing'. Here are some examples:

Non so cosa è successo.	I don't know what happened.
Sai che cosa ha fatto?	Do you know what he did?
Lei non sa guidare.	She does not know how to drive.

Ho conosciuto tuo zio.	I met your uncle.
Ci siamo conosciuti ieri.	We met yesterday.
Lui conosce bene Modena.	He knows Modena well.
Lei conosce le opere di Puccini?	Do you know the operas by Puccini?

As you can see from the examples:

sapere is to know how to do something (as a result of learning how to do it): *so, sai, sa, sappiamo, sapete, sanno.*

So guidare.	I know how to drive a car.
Sapevo cucinare.	I used to know how to cook.

conoscere is to know a person, thing or place (to recognise by seeing, hearing, tasting or touching): *conosco, conosci, conosce, conosciamo, conoscete, conoscono.*

Lo conosco.	I know him.
Lo conoscevo.	I knew him.

> To express the idea of how long you have been doing something, e.g. knowing a person, Italian uses the present tense, not the past, as in the following examples:
>
> | | |
> |---|---|
> | Conosciamo questa famiglia da tre anni. | 'We have known this family for three years'. (literally 'since three years ago') |
> | So guidare da cinque mesi. | 'I have been able (known how to) drive for five months'. (literally 'since five months ago') |

V Which part of which verb are you going to use? (you might wish to try more than one tense.)

a (Io) _____ il signor Pacelli da dieci anni.
b Mio figlio _____ suo figlio.
c I nostri figli _____ usare la posta elettronica.
d (Noi) _____ bene la famiglia Pacelli.
e Mia moglie _____ la signora Pacelli due anni fa. (perfect)
f I miei genitori _____ suo padre. (imperfect)
g Mio padre _____ bene la regione dove abitavano. (imperfect)
h Mia moglie ed io non _____ spedire messaggi di posta elettronica.
i I miei genitori non _____ usare il telefonino.
j Mia figlia _____ spedire delle foto con il suo telefonino.
k Io non _____ mandare delle foto via posta elettronica.

1.9.5 Impersonal verbs

These are expressions in which there is no particular subject; they include many common, everyday expressions such as time, and weather.

Weather expressions such as:

fa caldo	it is hot
piove	it is raining
nevica	it is snowing
è nuvoloso	it is cloudy

Time expressions such as:

che ora è?	what time is it?
è l'una	it is one o'clock
sono le due e mezza/mezzo	it is half-past two

Other common impersonal expressions such as:

bisogna	it is necessary
basta	it is enough
manca	(we) need, there's ... missing
si tratta di	it's a question of ...
sembra che	it seems that
ci vuole	it takes ...

VI How would you say these in Italian?

a It rains a lot in the UK.
b It is hot in Italy.
c It is 12 noon.
d It is 9.15.
e It's necessary to rest!
f We need some bread.
g It seems to be the motor.
h It takes a day to get to Italy.

1.9.6 'Back-to-front' verbs

Piacere, interessare and one or two others are used with the object liked, loved etc. as the subject:

Mi piace prendere un caffè alle dieci	I like to have a coffee at ten o'clock
Mi piacciono i vini italiani	I like Italian wines
Non mi interessa il golf	I am not interested in golf
Mi interessano le auto	I am interested in cars

Note how an infinitive is the subject in the first one, and how the verb has to be third person plural when a plural thing is liked etc.

Write five sentences saying what you like and don't like, and another five saying what you are and are not interested in. Make sure you have examples of singulars and plurals, and then learn them.

1.9.7 'To take', 'to bring' and 'to look for/fetch/meet' a person

These English verbs can be translated in various ways using *prendere* and *portare*; here are some examples of each.

prendere	to take transport, a drink and things in general, to fetch/meet
prendo l'autobus	I am taking the bus
prendiamo una birra?	shall we have (take) a beer?
è andato a prenderla alla stazione	he went to meet her at/fetch her from the station
portare	to carry, wear, bring, fetch, take something/somebody somewhere
porta una camicia rossa	he's wearing a red shirt
porta una borsa di cuoio	she's carrying a leather handbag
portami un bicchiere di vino	bring me a glass of wine
voglio portare il mio orologio alla spiaggia	I want to take my watch to the beach
ho portato i bambini alla piscina	I took the children to the swimming-pool
non portare via la tazza	don't take the cup away
una pizza da portar via	a take-away pizza

Note also *cercare*, 'to look for' (and 'to try to')

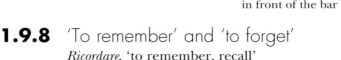

cerco una casa senza giardino	I'm looking for a house without a garden
vi cercherò davanti al bar	I'll look out for you in front of the bar

1.9.8 'To remember' and 'to forget'

Ricordare, 'to remember, recall'

Ricordo che tu eri a casa.	I remember that you were at home.
Ricordi il suo indirizzo?	Do you remember her address?

This verb holds no surprises, but the reflexive form can also be used when more of an 'effort to remember' is implied, especially remembering people:

Ricordarsi di, 'to remember' (literally 'to remind yourself of something/someone/of doing something'). In Italian, you remind yourself of something.

Mi ricordo di Marco.	I remember Marco.
Non ti ricordi di me?	Don't you remember me?
Ricordati di comprare il pane.	Remember to buy bread.

Dimenticare, 'to forget':

| Preferisco dimenticare il mio incidente. | I prefer to forget about my accident. |
| Hai dimenticato la lettera. | You have forgotten / left the letter behind. |

Dimenticarsi, 'to forget about something/doing something'

| Non mi dimenticherò di te. | I won't forget you. |
| Ti sei dimenticato di chiudere la porta!. | You've forgotten to shut the door! |

VII How would you say:

a I remember John.
b He remembers me.
c He remember my house.
d We both remember the holidays.
e I have forgotten my wife.
f I don't remember her smile.
g My children have not forgotten their mother.

1.9.9 Negative expressions

Negative statements include saying what you don't do, and expressions with 'no', 'nothing', 'never', 'nobody', etc.

Negations often start with 'no' as the first word in the sentence. You have already seen how *non* is put in front of the verb to express 'not'.

No, I don't know.	No, non so.
I don't speak Italian.	Non parlo italiano.
I don't eat meat.	Non mangio carne.
He doesn't drink wine.	Lui non beve vino.
They don't live in Ancona.	Non abitano ad Ancona.
You aren't married?	Lei non è sposato/a?

Some negative expressions are 'double negatives': *non* goes in front of the verb, and the other negative word after the verb.

non ... mai, 'never':

| Lei non è mai andata a Capri. | She has never been to Capri. |

non ... niente, 'nothing/not anything':

Non ho fatto niente.	I didn't do anything.

non ... nessuno/a, 'nobody/no one/no' ...:

Non ha visto nessuno.	He didn't see anyone.
Non veniva nessuno.	Nobody was coming.
Non avete nessuna obiezione?	Don't you have any objections?

Nessuno is shortened to *nessun* before masculine nouns.

Nessun errore.	No mistakes.

> The idea of 'any' in 'not any' or ' no ...' is not translated: *non ho tempo,* 'I haven't any time/I have no time'.

(*non ...*) *né ... né,* 'not ... either ... or'/'neither ... nor':

Non ho né tempo né soldi	I have neither time nor money.
Né mia sorella né mio fratello parlano l'italiano.	Neither my sister nor my brother speaks Italian.

> If you start with the main negative word you don't need the marker *non* in front of the verb:
> Nessuno è venuto.   Nobody came

VIII How would you say the following? If possible, say them aloud so that you can get used to the sound of them. Then cover up the English, read them again and think about the meaning. Finally cover up the Italian and translate the whole sentence.

a I have never been to Italy.   Io [__] sono [__] stato in Italia.
b They didn't hurt anyone.   Loro [__] hanno fatto male a [__].
c I never see Anna.   [__] vedo [__] Anna.
d They have nothing in   [__] hanno [__] nella loro casa.
   their house.
e You have never learned   [__] hai [__] imparato a nuotare?
   to swim?
f I don't see anybody.   Io [__] vedo [__].
g She never rides a bike.   Lei [__] va [__] in bicicletta.
h I have nothing in my pocket.   [__] ho [__] in tasca.
i I have never been to Massa   [__] sono [__] stato a Massa
   Carrara.   Carrara.
j Nobody is at home.   [__] è a casa.

IX Match up these sentences.

a We haven't anything to eat.

Non ho avuto tempo per andare in città.

b Nobody has been shopping.

Non c'è né pane né formaggio.

c I didn't have time to go to town.

Non ho soldi.

d There is no bread or cheese.

Non abbiamo niente da mangiare.

e You never go to the supermarket.

Nessuno ha fatto la spesa.

f I haven't any money.

Non vai mai al supermercato.

 Remember, there is no need for 'any' after a negative in Italian.

1.9.10 Question words and word order

Come?	How?
Dove?	Where?
Quando?	When?
Perché?	Why?
Quanto/a/i/e?	How much/many?
Quanto tempo?	How long?
Che?	What?/Which?
Che cosa?/Cosa?	What?
Chi?	Who?
Quale?	Which?

After these question words you invert the order of the subject and the verb if a separate subject is expressed – otherwise the verb follows the question word, as in the examples. (See section 1.3.2.)

Dove andate?	Where are you going?
Come va a Grosseto?	How is he going to Grosseto?
Perché è in Germania?	Why is she in Germany?
Quando partite?	When are you leaving?
Che cosa fate voi?	What are you doing?
Chi conoscono Loro?	Who do you know?
Quante camere avete?	How many bedrooms do you have?
Cosa farai?	What are you going to do?

X Which question word would you use?

a _____ abita il signor Vincenzo?
b _____ si chiama sua moglie?
c _____ partono per Londra?
d _____ vanno a Londra?
e _____ faranno a Londra?

f _____ ha un appuntamento in banca?
g _____ giorni staranno a Londra?
h _____ conosce a Londra?

1.9.11 'Since', 'ago' and 'to have just ...': *da, fa* and *appena*

Da, 'since' (also 'from' etc.)

With this expression you use a different tense in Italian from the one you would expect to use in English. In English, when we want to say we have been doing something for a certain length of time, we use the perfect tense. In Italian, we have to say they have been doing it since (a year etc.) and still are, so the present tense is used.

Abito qui da sei anni.	I have lived here for six years.
Impara l'italiano da due anni.	He has been learning Italian for two years.
Ho questa macchina da un anno.	I have had this car a year.
Aspettano da un'ora.	They have been waiting an hour.
Sono qui da due giorni.	I have been here two days.

XI How would you answer these questions? Remember to use the present tense in your answers.

a Da quanto tempo abiti qui?
b Da quanto tempo impari l'italiano?
c Da quanto tempo conosci il/la tuo/tua migliore amico/amica?

Fa, 'ago'

To express the idea of a certain amount of time ago, simply use an expression of time followed by *fa.*

Sono partito due anni fa.	I left two years ago.
Siete arrivati poco fa.	You have only just arrived.

Appena: used to express 'to have just'

In Italian, use this adverb (normal meaning 'hardly/scarcely') to express the idea of a very recent action. For current situations, use the perfect with it; if related to a situation in the past, use the imperfect.

Sono appena arrivato a casa.	I have just got in.
Ha appena telefonato.	He has just rung.
Abbiamo appena guardato un film molto brutto.	We have just seen a dreadful film.
La mia ragazza era appena arrivata.	My girlfriend had just arrived.
Avevamo appena sentito la notizia.	We had just heard the news.

XII How would you translate:

a Pino è *appena* arrivato a casa.
b Il mio amico ha *appena* telefonato.
c Abbiamo *appena* cenato.
d I miei genitori hanno *appena* venduto la loro casa.
e Ho *appena* finito il mio lavoro.

1.9.12 ▶Fast track: more on *avere* and other useful verbs

In Italian there are some expressions which use *avere* where we use the verb 'to be' in English. The most common ones are:

Ho … anni	I am … years (old)
Ho paura	I am afraid
Ho caldo/freddo	I am hot/cold
Ho fame/sete	I am hungry/thirsty
Ho ragione	I am right

Here are some other useful expressions based on verbs:

c'è/ci sono	there is/there are
c'era/c'erano	there was/were

How to say 'bring/take/fetch':

prendere	to take – prendo l'autobus
portare	to take/bring (someone/thing)

How to say 'to remember/recall'

ricordare	to remember
ricordarsi di	to remember (lit: to remind yourself of someone/something/doing something)
dimenticare	to forget
dimenticarsi	to forget about

A Negatives

Non is used by itself for straight negation ('I have not' …), whilst *No* is used to start a sentence.

Where other negative expressions are used, *non* is put in front of the verb and *niente/nulla, nessuno/a, mai* and *né … né* come after the verb.

non … niente/nulla	nothing
non … nessuno/a	nobody
non … mai	never

Non fanno niente	They aren't doing anything
Non ho mai nuotato lì	I have never swum there
Non ho visto nessuno	I didn't see anyone

B   Question words

These words introduce a question:

Quando?	When?
Perché?	Why?
Quanto/a/i/e?	How much/many?
Quanto tempo?	How long?
Che/Cosa/Che cosa?	What?
Chi?	Who?
Quale?	Which?

The subject (where there is one expressed) and verb are inverted after a question word.

Quando va tuo padre ad Alassio?
Dove vai tu?

C   *Da* and *appena*

Da has several meanings, including 'since'. You use *da* to answer the question 'how long'?

Da quanto tempo abiti in Calabria?	How long have you lived in Calabria?
Abito lì da dieci anni.	I have lived there ten years. (literally: I live there since 10 years).

In Italian the answer is in the present tense because you still live there.

Appena used to express 'to have just'

Sono appena arrivato.	I have just arrived. (I have scarcely arrived.)
Lo ha appena fatto.	He has (only) just done it. (He has hardly done it.)

In Italian you use the present tense because you are 'probably still doing it'.

2 NOUNS AND DETERMINERS

How to recognise nouns and determiners

▶▶ **If you know what nouns and determiners are, go on to 2.2.**

Nouns are naming words. They tell you who somebody is (e.g. 'he is a soldier', 'she is a mother') or what something is (e.g. 'it is a table', 'it is a rainbow').

 You can recognize nouns because you can say 'a' or 'the' in front of them – e.g. a pencil, the dog, a house, the postman.

Sometimes in English the same word can be a noun or a verb.

to drink – the drink
to walk – the walk

I There are 10 nouns in this text. Can you find them all?

> My sister has her own restaurant. She goes to the market each morning to buy fresh vegetables to make the soup for lunch. The other dishes she has prepared the night before and left ready to cook in the fridge.

A determiner is a word which comes in front of a noun to tell you (determine) which one it is:

the coat; a coat; my coat; your coat, this coat, which coat?

2.1 Nouns and gender

▶▶ **If you know about the gender of nouns go on to 2.2.**

In Italian all nouns are either masculine or feminine.

The word for 'bottle', *bottiglia*, is a feminine word.

The word for 'garden', *giardino*, is a masculine word.

Feminine nouns are usually indicated by *nf* in the dictionary (n = noun f = feminine) and masculine words by *nm*.

2.2 Nouns and the word for 'the': *il*, *la*, etc.

The word 'the' is a determiner. It is also called the definite article because it refers to a definite thing, e.g. the house you live in and not just any house.

▶▶ **If you know about *il* and *la* and the gender of nouns, go on to 2.3.**

2.2.1 Singular nouns

• The word for 'the' in front of singular masculine nouns is usually *il*:

| il ragazzo | the boy |
| il treno | the train |

• The word for 'the' in front of singular feminine nouns is usually *la*:

| la ragazza | the girl |
| la porta | the door |

• The word for 'the' in front of singular masculine and feminine words beginning with a vowel is *l'*:

| l'uomo | the man |
| l'acqua | the water |

• The word for 'the' in front of a fairly small group of singular masculine nouns beginning with the letters *z*, *gn*, *x*, *pn*, *ps*, *i/y* with a vowel, or *s* with a consonant, is *lo*.

| lo specchio | the mirror |
| lo gnocco | the dumpling |

I Put the correct form (*il*, *lo*, *l'* or *la*) in front of these.

a _____ macchina (f)	car
b _____ oliva (f)	olive
c _____ panino (m)	sandwich
d _____ penna (f)	ballpoint pen, biro
e _____ città (f)	town, city
f _____ squash (m)	squash (sport, not drink!)
g _____ uscita (m)	exit
h _____ autostrada (f)	motorway
i _____ ferrovia (f)	railway
j _____ sport (m)	sport
k _____ biglietto (m)	ticket

II Now do the same for these places.

a _____ casa (f)   house
b _____ farmacia (f)   chemist's
c _____ stazione (f)   station
d _____ strada (f)   street
e _____ sottopassaggio (m)   subway
f _____ parcheggio (m)   car park
g _____ banca (f)   bank
h _____ negozio (m)   shop
i _____ ufficio postale (m)   post office
j _____ ponte (m)   bridge

III Fill in the gaps with *il, l', lo* or *la.*

a _____ olio (m)   oil
b _____ gelato (m)   ice cream
c _____ nocciola (f)   hazelnut
d _____ bagno (m)   bathroom
e _____ insalata (f)   salad
f _____ ufficio (m)   office
g _____ burro (m)   butter
h _____ spazzola (f)   brush
i _____ zio (m)   uncle
j _____ zanzara (f)   mosquito
k _____ pranzo (m)   lunch
l _____ viaggio (m)   journey
m _____ acqua (f)   water
n _____ succo (m)   juice
o _____ uomo (m)   man
p _____ carta (f)   paper, map
q _____ scuola (f)   school
r _____ mano (f)   hand
s _____ finestra (f)   window
t _____ pollo (m)   chicken

2.3 Nouns in the plural: *i, gli* and *le*

▶▶ **If you know about the plural go on to 2.4.**

In the plural, the word for 'the' with all feminine words is *le.* The word for 'the' with most masculine nouns is *i.* With the group of masculine nouns beginning with *z, gn, x, pn, ps* etc., it is *gli.*

Singular	Plural
la casa	le case
il treno	i treni
lo gnocco	gli gnocchi

To make the plural of the noun in English, we usually add an -*s*. Italian nouns are not so simple, because they come more directly from Latin, which had a wide variety of ways of forming plurals. Here is a list of the main ways of forming Italian plurals. The first two ways of making plurals cover the majority of nouns, but there are plenty of the other kinds.

Masculine nouns which end in -*o* or -*a* form their plural with an -*i*:

il vino (**wine**)	i vini
il sistema (**system**)	i sistemi

Feminine nouns which end in -*a* form their plural with an -*e*:

la ragazza (**girl**)	le ragazze
la tavola (**table**)	le tavole

All nouns (both masculine and feminine) which end in -*e* form their plural with an -*i*:

il carabiniere (**Italian gendarme**)	i carabinieri
la luce (**light**)	le luci

Nouns of both genders which end in -*co* or -*ca,* or -*go* or -*ga,* add an *h* in the plural before the *c* or the *g,* to stop the *c* or *g* becoming soft (i.e. sounding like *ch* or *j* in English):

il lago (**lake**)	i laghi
lo scacco (**chequer**)	gli scacchi
l'amica (**female friend**)	le amiche (**but see** l'amico **below**)

However, there are a few exceptions. With a few nouns, the *h* is left out, and so the *c* or *g* does become soft, and is pronounced like *ch* or *j*. A good demonstration of this is the family name *Medici,* which actually means 'doctors'.

l'amico (**male friend**)	gli amici
il medico (**doctor**)	i medici

A small number of feminine nouns ending in -*o,* -*i,* -*ie* and those ending with accented -*à* or -*ù* stay the same in the plural. There are some common exceptions among feminine nouns ending in -*ie* such as: *la moglie > le mogli.*

l'auto (car)	le auto
la moto (motor bike)	le moto
la città (town)	le città

A small number of masculine nouns stay the same in the plural, including all those ending in a consonant or an accented vowel.

l'autobus (bus)	gli autobus
il bar (bar)	i bar
lo sci (ski)	gli sci
il ragù (meat sauce)	i ragù

A group of masculine nouns become feminine in the plural, ending in -a or -e.

l'uovo (egg)	le uova
il braccio (arm)	le braccia
l'orecchio (ear)	le orecchie or gli orecchi
il ginocchio (knee)	le ginocchia
il dito (finger)	le dita
mille (thousand)	due mila (two thousand)

Some plurals are just irregular and have to be learned. Fortunately there are not many of them. In the case of words ending in -*ccia* and -*ggia*, both words lose the penultimate -*i* because it is not needed to soften the *cc* and *gg*, as the -*e* which replaces it does the same job.

la moglie (wife)	le mogli
l'uomo (man)	gli uomini
la faccia (face)	le facce
la spiaggia (beach)	le spiagge
la mano (hand)	le mani

To sum up, the majority of nouns form their plurals as follows:

Masculine		Feminine	
Singular	**Plural**	**Singular**	**Plural**
-o	-i	-a	-e

Masculine/feminine	
Singular	**Plural**
-e	-i

I Put these words into the plural.

a	il cane	the dog
b	il gatto	the cat
c	la barca	the boat

d la terrazza	the terrace	
e la macchina	the car	
f la moto	the motor-bike	
g il castello	the castle	
h il tedesco	the German	
i il pacco	the packet	

2.4 Nouns and the word for 'a': *un, un', uno* and *una*

The word 'a' is a determiner. It is also called the indefinite article because it refers to any one item and not a specific one: a bottle of red wine, not *the* bottle that you have chosen specifically.

▶▶ **If you know about *un, uno* and *una* go on to 2.5.**

- The word for 'a' in front of masculine nouns is usually *un*.

  un battello   a ferry boat

- The word for 'a' in front of masculine nouns beginning with *z, gn, x, pn, ps, i/y* with a vowel, or *s* with a consonant is *uno*.

  uno sportello   a trap-door, ticket window

- The word for 'a' in front of feminine noun is *una*.

  una pizza   a pizza

If the feminine noun begins with a vowel, the article is *un'*.

un'amica   a female friend
un'idea   an idea

I Imagine you are talking about your family and pets. How would you say you have one of all these? Choose between *un, un', uno* and *una*.

Ho ...

a	_____ fratello		**f**	_____ zia
b	_____ sorella		**g**	_____ cugino
c	_____ nonno		**h**	_____ cugina
d	_____ nonna		**i**	_____ figlia
e	_____ zio		**j**	_____ cane

In Italian, you omit the indefinite article when talking about occupations, jobs, religions, nationality, etc.

Sono studente.	I am a student.
È americano.	He is American.
Gino è medico.	Gino is a doctor.
Sei cattolico?	Are you a Catholic?

Some nouns have a masculine and a feminine form. The masculine form usually ends in -*o*, and to make the feminine form you usually replace the -*o* with an -*a*. Sometimes there is a separate word for the feminine and masculine forms and sometimes the word is the same, just with a different article, e.g *il tassista/la tassista*.

un amico, un'amica	a friend
un dottore, una dottoressa	a doctor
un attore, un'attrice	an actor, an actress
un cantante, una cantante	a singer
un padre, una madre	a father, a mother
un marito, una moglie	a husband, a wife
un figlio, una figlia	a son, a daughter

II How would you say ...

a Vittorio is a doctor.
b Chiara is a student.
c Ermenegildo is a teacher.
d Toni is an American.
e Enrico is a Catholic.
f He is unemployed.
g She is a car driver.

 The words for *a* are also known as the indefinite article, because they are used to talk about *one* thing but not any particular one.

They are used with singular nouns: *Ho un appartamento/Ho una casa*.

To talk about more than one thing in English we say 'some' or 'any', and sometimes we just miss out the word completely:

He's got some flats.	Ha degli appartamenti.
Has he got any farms?	Ha delle fattorie?
He hasn't got any houses.	Non ha case.

Sometimes you can just miss out the word for 'any', particularly in negative sentences:

I haven't got (any) time	Non ho tempo
I haven't got (any) money	Non ho soldi

In Italian, you often need to use a word for 'some' or 'any' with a plural positive sentence, and the word for 'some' or 'any' has to agree with the noun in the sentence. Here are the words you need to use:

Masc. pl (most words)	Masc. pl. beginning with *z, gn, x, pn, ps, i/y,* with a vowel, or with *s* with a consonant	Fem. pl. (all words)
dei	degli	delle

	Singular	Plural
Ha …	un giardino	dei fiori
	un prato	degli alberi
	una casa	delle piante
S/he has got …	a garden	some flowers
	a lawn	some trees
	a house	some plants
Non ha …	un garage	alberi da frutta
	uno studio	olmi
	una piscina	rose
S/he hasn't got …	a garage	any fruit trees
	a study	any elms
	a pool	any roses

III Complete the sentences with *un, uno, una, dei, degli* or *delle*.

a Il mio amico abita in _____ grande condominio.
b Ha _____ piccolo appartamento al quarto piano.
c Ha _____ bella sala da pranzo.
d Ha _____ piccolo alcone dove tiene la bicicletta.
e Sul balcone ci sono anche _____ piante in ___ vasi da fiori.
f Nella sua camera ci sono _____ armadio, _____ libri, _____ sedie e _____ specchi.
g Ha _____ CD e _____ videogiochi, ma non ha _____ lettore di DVD.
h C'è _____ solo ascensore, ma è sempre rotto.

2.5 How to tell if a noun is masculine or feminine

It is not always possible to tell whether a word is masculine or feminine in Italian unless you already know it. It is helpful to learn nouns along with their word for 'the' (*il* or *la*). There are also some other ways of working out if a word is masculine or feminine:

If you hear il, lo, un or uno being used in front of it, it is masculine.
If you hear la or una being used in front of it, it is feminine (but if you hear l' it could be either).
If you hear i, gli or le being used in front of it, it is plural.

The word for 'a' in front of feminine nouns beginning with a vowel is usually *un*:

un'arancia	an orange

In addition to this, there are some rules – but there are also a lot of exceptions!

As a rule, most nouns ending in *-o* are masculine and most nouns ending in *-a* are feminine.

il treno	train
la macchina	car

These endings also usually indicate that a noun is masculine:

-ore/-tore	il professore (**teacher**), l'autore (**author**)
-ere/-iere	l'ingegnere (**engineer**), il carabiniere (Italian gendarme)
-ame/-ale/-ile	il falegname (**carpenter**), il giornale (**newspaper**), il missile (**missile**)

The following endings usually mean that a noun is feminine:

-ione	la soluzione	(solution)
-tà	la bontà	(goodness)
-tù	la gioventù	(youth)
-udine	la solitudine	(solitude)
-igine	l'origine	(origin)
-ite	la laringite	(laryngitis)
-ice	l'attrice	(actress)
-i	la crisi	(crisis)
-ie	la serie	(series)

Some nouns have a masculine and a feminine form:

il figlio	la figlia	(son/daughter)
il nonno	la nonna	(grandfather/grandmother)
lo scrittore	la scrittrice	(writer)
il cameriere	la cameriera	(waiter/waitress)
il dottore	la dottoressa	(doctor)
l'attore	l'attrice	(actor/actress)

I   Now put the correct form of *il*, *l'*, *lo* or *la* in front of these words. The rules above will help you.

a	_____ emozione	**k**	_____ pinacoteca
b	_____ scarpa	**l**	_____ tangenziale
c	_____ seggio	**m**	_____ autostrada
d	_____ enoteca	**n**	_____ città
e	_____ manifestazione	**o**	_____ negozio
f	_____ albergo	**p**	_____ carta
g	_____ zanzara	**q**	_____ fiasco
h	_____ zucchero	**r**	_____ barca
i	_____ sporco	**s**	_____ pasta
j	_____ spiedo	**t**	_____ vaporetto

2.6   How to say 'my', 'your', 'his', 'her', etc.

▶▶ **If you know about these words, go on to 2.6.8.**

These are words for saying what belongs to whom: 'my coat', 'his umbrella', 'your briefcase', 'their house', 'our cat', etc.

In English, we only have one form of each: 'my', 'your', 'his', 'her', 'our', 'their'. In Italian, there are singular and plural and masculine and feminine forms to agree with their nouns.

	Masc. sg.	**Fem. sg.**	**Masc. pl.**	**Fem. pl.**
my	il mio	la mia	i miei	le mie
your (familiar singular)	il tuo	la tua	i tuoi	le tue
your (formal)	il suo	la sua	i suoi	le sue
his/her/its	il suo	la sua	i suoi	le sue
our	il nostro	la nostra	i nostri	le nostre
your (familiar plural)	il vostro	la vostra	i vostri	le vostre
your (formal plural)	il loro	la loro	i loro	le loro
their (masc and fem)	il loro	la loro	i loro	le loro

2.6.1   'My': *il mio, la mia, i miei, le mie*

The word for 'my' agrees in number and gender with the person or thing it is describing. This means that you use the masculine form *il mio* with masculine nouns and the feminine form *la mia* with feminine nouns.

il mio giardino	my garden
la mia segretaria	my secretary
il mio cane	my dog

Note that the definite article *il, la, l'* is omitted before members of the family in the singular, unless the word is accompanied by an adjective or modified (*il mio fratello minore, il mio fratellino*):

| mio fratello | my brother |
| mia madre | my mother |

'My' in front of plural nouns is *i miei* for masculine and *le mie* for feminine. The definite article *i/le* is always used.

| i miei gatti | my cats |
| le mie sorelle | my sisters |

I *Il mio* or *la mia?*

a _____ gatto	**f** _____ casa
b _____ valigia	**g** _____ amica
c _____ mamma	**h** _____ tessera
d _____ papà	**i** _____ cane
e _____ libro	**j** _____ macchina

II Now do the same for these plurals.

a _____ conigli	**f** _____ giacche
b _____ case	**g** _____ pesche
c _____ battelli	**h** _____ giardini
d _____ maglie	**i** _____ occhi
e _____ amici	**j** _____ denti

III ... and your family. Imagine you are showing someone photographs of your family. What would you say?

Ecco il mio/ i miei .../ Ecco la mia/ le mie ...

a bambini	**e** madre	**i** nonno
b marito	**f** sorella	**j** cugine
c moglie	**g** fratelli	**k** cugino
d padre	**h** nonna	

2.6.2 'Your': *il tuo, la tua, i tuoi, le tue*

If you are not going to need this, go on to 2.6.3.

Il tuo/la tua etc. agrees in gender and number with its noun, like *il mio* etc., and behaves in the same way. You can only use these forms when speaking to a child or someone that you know very well (the familiar singular form).

IV Put the correct form of *tuo/il tuo, tua/la tua, i tuoi* or *le tue* in front of these words.

È il tuo/la tua … Sono i tuoi/le tue …

a bambini	**e** fratello	**i** cane
b padre	**f** genitori	**j** gatti
c madre	**g** figlio	
d sorelle	**h** figlie	

V   How would you ask what they are called?

Come si chiama il tuo/la tua…? Come si chiamano il tuoi/le tue…?

a colleghe	**e** amici	**i** genitori
b collega	**f** amica	**j** madre
c amico	**g** fratello	
d amiche	**h** sorelle	

Note that *collega* (NOT *collego*) can be either masculine or feminine, like many nouns in -*a*, like *il/la giornalista*, *l'artista*.

2.6.3   'His' and 'her': *il suo, la sua, i suoi, le sue*

▶▶   **If you know about *il suo, la sua,* etc. go on to 2.6.4.**

The words for 'his/her' rhyme with *il tuo/la tua* etc., and are used in the same way.

Note:

suo fratello means both 'his brother' and 'her brother';

sua sorella means both 'his sister' and 'her sister';

i suoi amici means both 'his friends' and 'her friends'.

VI   *Parla di Luigi.* Talk about Luigi by filling in the right word (*suo/il suo/ sua/la sua/i suoi/le sue*).

a _____ amiche si chiamano Maria e Giulia.

b _____ cugino si chiama Giuseppe.

c _____ fratello è grande.

d _____ madre è scultrice.

e _____ padre lavora alla Banca d'Italia.

f _____ sorelle sono professoresse.

g _____ fratello minore ha solo otto anni.

h _____ sport preferito è il tennis.

i _____ piatti preferiti sono la pizza Quattro Stagioni e gli spaghetti alla Carbonara.

j _____ colore preferito è il blu scuro.

Not sure whether *colore* is (m) or (f)? Look for a clue in the sentence: *preferito*.

VII *Parla di Gabriella.* Now do the same for Gabriella's family and friends.

a _____ amica si chiama Filomena.
b _____ nonno si chiama Flavio.
c _____ fratelli si chiamano Enrico e Bruno.
d _____ sorella si chiama Bianca.
e Come si chiamano _____ genitori?
f _____ monopattino è nero e giallo.
g _____ passatempo preferito è il pattinaggio.
h _____ colori preferiti sono il rosso e il bianco.
i _____ piatto preferito sono gli spaghetti.
j _____ bevande preferite sono la grappa e la birra.

2.6.4 'Our': *il nostro, la nostra, i nostri, le nostre*

▶▶ **Know about *il nostro, la nostra,* etc.? Go on to 2.6.5.**

The words for 'our' are *nostro/nostra* and *nostri/nostre*. Like the other words you have met so far, they change in the singular, plural, masculine and feminine: *il nostro appartamento, la nostra casa, i nostri cani, le nostre macchine.*

VIII How would you say these are *our* things?

È il nostro/la nostra … Sono i nostri/le nostre …

a casa   **e** vini   **i** albero
b appartamento   **f** capannone   **j** camere
c cani   **g** macchina
d negozio   **h** giardino

2.6.5 'Your': *il vostro, la vostra, i vostri, le vostre*

The word for 'your' (familiar plural form) is easy to remember because it rhymes with *il nostro/la nostra* and *i nostri/le nostre* and behaves in the same way: *vostro figlio, le vostre sorelle.*

IX Ask if these are *your* things.

È il vostro/la vostra … Sono i vostri/le vostre …

a officina?   **e** pantaloni?   **i** lettera?
b sedia?   **f** guanti?   **j** chiavi?
c matite?   **g** ombrello?
d libri?   **h** roba?

2.6.6 'Their': *il loro, la loro, i loro, le loro*

The word for 'their' is *il/la/i/le loro*. Unlike the other possessives, this word is invariable – although the article before it changes according to gender and number, the word *loro* doesn't.

X Say these are their things.

È il/la loro ... Sono i/le loro ...

a macchina
b garage
c biciclette
d giardino
e fiori
f piante
g casa
h porta
i finestre
j balcone

2.6.7 'Your' (formal): *il suo, la sua, i suoi, le sue; il loro, la loro, i loro, le loro*

The word for 'your' (formal form – for talking to strangers, people older than you, etc.) is the same form as the word for 'his/her' (*il suo, la sua, i suoi, le sue*), and works the same way. For the formal plural 'your', the word is the same as 'their' (*il loro, la loro, i loro* and *le loro*). Sometimes, in more formal writing, the initial *s* or *l* is capitalized (*il Suo, la Loro*, etc.).

XI Ask if these are *your* things, using the formal form *il suo, la sua, i suoi, le sue.*

È il suo/la sua .../Sono i suoi/le sue ...

a gatto?
b sedia?
c libri?
d piedi?
e giacca?
f tazze?
g fratelli?
h moto?
i camera?
j matita?

2.6.8 ▶Fast track: nouns and determiners

All nouns in Italian are either masculine or feminine.

The word for 'the' with masculine singular nouns is *il*.
The word for 'the' with masculine singular nouns that begin with *z*,
   gn, *x*, *pn*, *ps*, *i/y* with a vowel, or *s* with a consonant, is *lo*.
The word for 'the' with feminine singular nouns is *la*.
The word for 'the' with singular nouns of either gender that begin
   with a vowel is *l'*.
The word for 'the' with masculine plural nouns is *i*.
The word for 'the' with masculine plural nouns that begin with *z*, *gn*,
   x, *pn*, *ps*, *i/y* with a vowel, or *s* with a consonant, is *gli*.
The word for 'the' with feminine plural nouns is *le*.

The word for 'a' with masculine nouns is *un*.
The word for 'a' with masculine nouns that begin with *z*, *gn*, *x*, *pn*, *ps*,
   i/y with a vowel, or *s* with a consonant, is *uno*.
The word for 'a' with feminine nouns is *una*.
The word for 'a' with feminine nouns that begin with a vowel is *un'*.

To say what people *are* or *do* (their jobs, nationalities, etc.)
you often omit the *a* in Italian:

Sono studente.   I am (a) student.

'A' does not have a plural of its own. The plural of 'a' in
English would be 'some' or 'any'. In Italian it is sometimes
missed out, but usually it is rendered as *dei*, *degli* or *delle*
according to the gender and type of the noun it is with:

Cerco dei libri.   I am looking for some books.
Non cerco libri/nessun libro.   I am not looking for (any)
                             books.

It is a good idea to learn Italian nouns with 'the' (*il* and *la*):
la strada; *il gatto*.

How to translate 'my', 'your', 'his', 'her', 'its', etc.:

	With sing. nouns		With pl. nouns	
	Masc.	**Fem.**	**Masc.**	**Fem.**
my	il mio	la mia	i miei	le mie
your (familiar singular)	il tuo	la tua	i tuoi	le tue
your (formal singular)	il suo	la sua	i suoi	le sue
his/her/its	il suo	la sua	i suoi	le sue
our	il nostro	la nostra	i nostri	le nostre
your (familiar plural)	il vostro	la vostra	i vostri	le vostre
their (masc. and fem.)	il loro	la loro	i loro	le loro
your (formal plural)	il loro	la loro	i loro	le loro

2.7 More determiners

Remember determiners are words which come before the nouns and say 'which' one it is. You already know some but there are some more.

Ones you already know: 'the table/a table/my table/your table'
New ones: 'which table?/all tables/the same table/
                                          several tables/some tables/every table' ....

If you do not think you need these yet, leave them and come back to them later.

il/la	the
un/uno/una/un'	a
il mio/la mia/i miei/le mie	my
questo/questa/questi/queste	this
quanto/quanta/quanti/quante?	how much/how many?
altro/altra/altri/altre	other
molto/molta/molti/molte	much, many
poco/poca/pochi/poche	(a) little, few
tanto/tanta/tanti/tante	so much/many
tutto/tutta/tutti/tutte	all or every
tutti/tutte e due OR entrambi/entrambe	both
certo/certa/certi/certe	(a) certain
troppo/troppa/troppi/troppe	too much, too many
stesso/stessa/stessi/stesse	same
qualche	some/any/a few
alcuni/alcune	some
nessun(o)/nessuna no(ne),	not any, no/none

2.7.1 'This', 'these', 'that' and 'those': *questo, questa, questi, queste, quel, quello, quella, quell', quei, quegli, quelle*

The demonstrative adjectives *questo/questa* etc. are used to point to a particular thing or things.

this page, these clothes, that book, those books

	Singular		Plural	
	Masc.	**Fem.**	**Masc.**	**Fem.**
this, these	questo	questa	questi	queste
that, those	quel, quello	quella, quell'	quei, quegli	quelle

Note that *questo* and *questa* become *quest'* in front of words beginning with a vowel, e.g. *quest'anno, quest'estate* and *quella* becomes *quell'* e.g. *quell'arancia*.

I Put the correct form in front of these words.

a _____ hotel è molto buono.	That hotel is very good.
b Di fronte a _____ casa, c'è un giardino.	In front of this house there is a garden.
c In _____ giardino crescono delle piante.	In this garden, some plants grow.
d _____ donne lavorano nel giardino.	These women work in the garden.
e _____ fiori sono rari.	Those flowers are rare.
f _____ albero è molto vecchio.	This tree is very old.
g _____ porta è riservata ai turisti.	That door is reserved for tourists.
h _____ riviste sono gratuite.	These magazines are free.
i _____ uomo fa delle foto.	That man is taking photographs.
j _____ primavera ci sono molti tromboncini.	This spring there are lots of daffodils.

2.7.2 'How much?', 'How many?': *quanto/ quanta/quanti/quante?*

Quanto/quanta/quanti/quante? mean 'how much?' or 'how many?', and agree in number and gender with the noun.

Singular		Plural	
Masc.	**Fem.**	**Masc.**	**Fem.**
quanto	quanta	quanti	quante

II Put the correct form of *quanto/quanta/quanti/quante* in front of these questions.

a _____ macchine ci sono nel parcheggio?
b _____ tipi di vino vengono prodotti qui?
c _____ anni hai?
d _____ vino vuoi?
e _____ latte c'è nel bicchiere?

2.7.3 'Some', 'other', 'all', 'any', 'every', etc.

These words agree as normal with the noun (but note that *qualche* is only used in the singular, even if it has a plural sense).

altro/altra/altri/altre, 'other'

Vuoi qualcos' altro?	Do you want something (anything) else?
Portami un altro bicchiere di vino!	Bring me another glass of wine!

molto/molta/molti/molte, 'much', 'many'

Ci vuole molto tempo.	It needs/takes a lot of time.
Ci sono molti pesci nel mare.	There are many fishes in the sea.

poco/poca/pochi/poche, '(a) little', 'few'

C'è poca gente qui.	There aren't many (= there are few) people here.
Ho pochi soldi.	I haven't got much (= I have got little) money.
Ci sono poche case nel villaggio.	There aren't many (= there are few) houses in the village.

tanto/tanta/tanti/tante, 'so much/many'

Ha tanti gatti!	S/he has so many cats!
Ci sono tante macchine in città!	There are so many cars in the city!

tutto/tutta/tutti/tutte, 'all' or 'every'

tutto il tempo	all the time
tutta la mia famiglia	all my family
tutti gli altri	all the others (m)
tutte le altre	all the others (f)
tutti i fiori	all the flowers/every flower
tutti i giorni	every day
tutte le settimane	every week

tutti/ tutte e due or *entrambi/ entrambe*, 'both'

su entrambi i lati	on both sides
Tutte e due/Tutt'e due erano qui.	They were both here.

certo/certa/certi/certe, '(a) certain'

una certa donna	a certain woman
un certo libro	a certain book
certi cani	certain dogs
certe ragazze	certain girls

troppo/troppa/troppi/troppe, 'too much', 'too many'

Ha mangiato troppo cioccolato.	He's had too much chocolate.
Abbiamo passato troppo tempo al sole.	We've spent too much time in the sun.
C'è troppa gente qui!	There are too many people here!
C'è troppa roba in casa!	There's too much stuff in the house!

stesso/stessa/stessi/stesse, 'same'

Siamo nella stessa casa.	We are in the same house.
lo stesso giorno	the same day
gli stessi ragazzi	the same boys

qualche, 'some/any/a few'

Note that *alcuno/alcuna/alcuni/alcune* can also be used to express 'some/any/a few'.

qualche tempo fa	some time ago
Ho qualche libro.	I have some books.
Ho alcune riviste.	I have some magazines.
C'è qualche macchina guasta.	There are some broken-down cars.

alcun(o)/alcuna, nessun(o)/nessuna, 'no/none', '(not) any'

Non ho nessun libro di Manzoni.	I have no books by Manzoni.
Non c'è nessuno qui.	There's no one here.

3 PRONOUNS

What is a pronoun?

A pronoun is a word which stands for a noun. Instead of saying:

Mr Jones	you can say	he: lui
the woman	you can say	she: lei
my husband/wife and I	you can say	we: noi
Mr and Mrs Brown	you can say	they: loro

In English instead of saying 'table' we say 'it'. In Italian the words for 'it', used with things, are *esso* (masculine) and *essa* (feminine).

Note: Don't forget that in Italian the subject pronouns are almost always missed out, because the ending on the verb does their job, and tells you who or what is the subject of the verb.

3.1 Io, tu, Lei, lui, lei, esso/essa, 'I', 'you', 'he', 'she', 'it': subject pronouns

▶▶ **If you know what a subject pronoun is, go on to 3.1.1.**

The subject is the person or thing who does the action.

I run, *you* play, *he* eats, *she* drinks, *it* shuts, *we* live, *you* swim, *they* talk

The subject pronouns in Italian are as follows:

	Singular	Plural
first person	io – I	noi – we
second person	tu – you	voi – you
	Lei – you (polite)	Loro – you (polite)
third person	lui/egli – he	loro – they
	lei/ella – she	
	esso/essa – it	

3.1.1 *Io*, 'I': first person singular

You use the first person when you are talking about yourself.

(Io) sono	I am ...
(Io) dormo	I am sleeping
(Io) bevo	I am drinking
(Io) ascolto	I am listening
(Io) mi chiamo Smith e (io) abito ...	I am called Smith and I live ...

Io is only written with a capital letter at the beginning of a sentence.

After *io* the verb usually ends in *-o* in the present tense.

3.1.2 *Tu*, 'you': second person singular, familiar form

You use *tu* when you are talking to one person you know very well, someone who has invited you to do so, or to a child.

Tu hai un cane?	Have you got a dog?
Tu sei andato a Roma?	Did you go to Rome?

After *tu* the verb ends in *-i* in the present tense.

3.1.3 *Lei*, 'you': second person singular, polite form

You use *Lei* when you are talking to one person you don't know very well, your boss at work, your teacher, someone who is older than you, etc. It translates 'you', but has the same form as the word for 'she', and is written with a capital in more formal writing, but can also be written without.

After *Lei* the verb ends in *-a* or *-e* in the present tense, except for *essere* (to be) which ends in *-è*.

Lei è insegnante?	Are you a teacher?
Lei è italiano, signor Rossi?	Are you Italian, Mr Rossi?

3.1.4 *Lui (egli)*, *lei (ella)* and *esso/essa*, 'he', 'she', 'it': third person singular

You use *lui/lei/esso/essa* when you are talking about someone or something else. They translate 'he', 'she' and 'it'.

Remember that in Italian everything is either masculine or feminine. A chair is feminine, so if you want to say anything about it, you have to use *essa* ('she'); similarly, a book is masculine so if you want to refer to it, you have to say *esso* ('he'). For people you use *lui* ('he') and *lei* ('she'). But don't forget that the pronouns are usually omitted anyway – you only use them for reinforcement, emphasis or contrast – e.g. *È tuo padre? – No, lui è mio padre.*

(Lui) è inglese.	He's English.
(Essa) è la mia macchina.	It's my car.
Aspetto mia zia. (Lei) arriva subito.	I'm waiting for my aunt. She's arriving soon.

After *lui/lei/esso/essa* the verb usually ends in *-a* or *-e* in the present tense.

3.1.5 *Noi*, 'we': first person plural

You use *noi* to talk about yourself and someone else. You use this word when you would use 'we' in English. As with the other pronouns, *noi* is usually omitted because the verb ending does its job for it.

(Noi) parliamo tedesco.	We speak German.
(Noi) mangiamo degli spaghetti.	We are eating spaghetti.
(Noi) non fumiamo, grazie.	We don't smoke, thanks.

After *noi* the verb always ends in *-iamo* in the present tense.

3.1.6 *Voi*, 'you': second person plural, familiar form

You use *voi* when you are talking to two or more people you know well, or who are younger than you, related to you, etc. It translates 'you'. *Voi* is often referred to as the 'familiar plural' form, as it is used in the plural when talking to people you know.

After *voi* the verb always ends in *-ate*, *-ete* or *-ite* in the present tense, according to whether the verb is an *-are* verb, an *-ere* one or an *-ire* one.

(Voi) mangiate cioccolato?	Do you eat chocolate?
(Voi) prendete il treno?	Are you taking the train?
(Voi) finite presto?	Are you finishing soon?

3.1.7 *Loro*, 'you': second person plural, polite form

You use *Loro* when you are talking to two or more people of either gender, whom you don't know, in a very formal context. It also translates 'you'.

After *Loro* the verb ends in *-ano*, *-ono* or *-anno* in the present tense.

3.1.8 *Loro*, 'they': third person plural

You use *loro* when you are talking about more than one person or thing.

It translates 'they'.

Noi siamo italiani, ma loro sono tedeschi.	We are Italians, but they are Germans.
Io ho due gatti, ma loro hanno un cane.	I have two cats, but they have a dog.

After *loro* the verb usually ends in *-ano, -ono* or *-anno* in the present tense.

I Which Italian subject pronoun should you use?

a I am going to the cinema tonight.
b After the cinema we are going to a restaurant.
c My girlfriends will be there.
d The house is very nice.
e Luca is playing.
f Isabel is going to watch.
g Where are you going?

II Which subject pronoun would you use in these sentences?

a Giovanni abita a Venezia. _____ prende spesso il vaporetto.
b I miei genitori si chiamano Luigi e Maria. _____ abitano a Como.
c _____ non siamo ancora pronti.
d Vieni anche _____?
e Mia sorella gioca a calcio. _____ gioca molto bene.
f Mi piace il tè. _____ bevo molto tè.
g Come si chiama questa ragazza? _____ è molto bella!
h _____ vi chiamate Giovanni e Paolo?
i _____ guidiamo una Fiat 500. Andiamo molto piano!
j Da dove venite ____?

3.1.9 ▶Fast track: subject pronouns

A pronoun is a word which stands for a noun:

I run, *you* play, *he* eats, *she* drinks, *it* shuts, *we* live, *you* swim, *they* talk

The subject is the person or thing who does the action.

Pronouns are usually omitted in Italian, but when you do use them (usually for emphasis or clarification), they are as follows:

You use *io* (first person singular) when you are talking about yourself.

After *io* the verb usually ends in *-o* in the present tense

You use *tu* (second person singular, familiar form) when you are talking to one person you know very well, someone who has invited you to do so, or to a child.

After *tu* the verb usually ends in *-i* in the present tense.

You use *Lei* when you are talking to one person you don't know very well, someone who is older than you, etc. It translates 'you'.

After *Lei* the verb usually ends in *-a* or *-e* in the present tense.

You use *lui/lei* and *esso/essa* (third person singular) to translate 'he', 'she' and 'it'.

In Italian everything is either masculine or feminine so the table (*la tavola*) is 'she' (*essa*) and the book (*il libro*) is 'he' (*esso*).

After *lui/lei* and *esso/essa* the verb usually ends in *-a* or *-e* in the present tense.

You use *noi* (first person plural) to talk about yourself and someone else. You use it when you would use 'we' in English.

After *noi* the verb usually ends in *-iamo* in the present tense.

You use *voi* (second person plural, familiar form) to translate 'you'.

Voi is often referred to as the 'plural familiar' form, as it is used in the plural when talking to friends or young people.

After *voi* the verb usually ends in *-ate, -ete* or *-ite* in the present tense.

You use *Loro* when you are talking in a very formal context to two or more people of either gender, whom you don't know, who are older than you, etc. It also translates 'you'.

Loro is often referred to as the 'plural polite' form, as it is used in the plural when talking to someone older than you or to strangers in a very formal context.

After *Loro* the verb usually ends in *-ano, -ono* or *-anno* in the present tense.

You use *loro* (third person plural) to translate 'they'.

After *loro* the verb usually ends in *-ano, -ono* or *-anno* in the present tense.

3.2 *Lo, la, li, le,* 'him', 'her', 'it', 'them': direct object pronouns

▶▶ **If you know what a direct object pronoun is and how to use it, go on to 3.2.1.**

'Him', 'her', 'it' and 'them' are called object pronouns. They are the person or object which has the action done to it.

I saw John.	him
John saw Karen.	her
I bought the watch.	it
I like Paul.	him
He likes Isabelle.	her
She doesn't like the boys.	them

In English it is easy to recognise the direct object as it always comes straight after the verb.

I Which is the direct object?

a I bought a new car.
b My husband drove it home for me.
c A dog chased a cat across the road.
d He swerved and hit a tree.
e He broke the wing mirror.
f He bought me a bunch of flowers.
g He took the car to the garage to be repaired.

3.2.1 *Lo, la, li, le*: 'him', 'her', 'it', 'them'; *La, Li, Le*: 'you'

The words for 'him/her' or 'it' in Italian are *lo* (masculine) and *la* (feminine), and the words for 'them' are *li* (masculine) and *le* (feminine). The words for 'you' (polite form) are *La* in the singular and *Li* in the plural. In Italian, the *lo, la, li* and *le* usually come in front of the verb. However, they can be attached to the end of the verb in certain cases (e.g. infinitive, imperatives, present participles, gerunds and the word *ecco*).

Eccolo!	There it/he is!
Li prendo.	I'm taking them.
aiutandola	helping her
Lo vedo.	I see it/him (m).

Lo and *la* become *l'* before words beginning with a vowel or *h*.

II Insert the correct direct object pronoun.

a I see her.	_____ vedo.
b She sees him.	_____ vede.
c We see them. (m)	_____ vediamo.
d I have it.	Ce _____ 'ho.
e I am helping* you. (polite form)	_____ aiuto.
f I am wearing* it. (m)	___ porto.

*These are present tenses, the pronoun goes before!

3.2.2 *Mi, ti, ci* and *vi*: 'me', 'you' and 'us'

These pronouns mean the same as 'me', 'you' and 'us' in English, and they also come in front of the verb.

Mi ha visto!	She's seen me!
Ti chiama!	He's calling you!
Ci vede.	He can see us.
Vi aiutiamo.	We're helping you.

3.2.3 ▶ **Fast track:** direct object pronouns

Lo, la, li, le, La, Le, Li, 'him', 'her', 'it', 'them', 'you': direct object pronouns

In English 'him', 'her', 'you', 'it', etc always come straight after the verb.

In Italian, the *lo, la, li, le, La, Le* and *Li* usually come in front of the verb, but they are sometimes attached to the end of it (e.g. infinitive, imperatives, present participles, gerunds and the word *ecco*).

Lo prendo.	I take it.
La vedo.	I see her.
Eccolo!	There it is!

Mi, ti, ci and *vi*: 'me', 'you' and 'us'

Like the other pronouns, these words usually come in front of the verb except after an infinitive, imperative, etc.

Arrivederci!	We'll meet (us) again!
Vi preghiamo di non parlare.	We ask you not to talk.
Mi ami?	Do you love me?
Ti odio!	I hate you!

3.3 *Mi, ti, gli, le, ci, vi, gli/loro,* 'to me', 'to you', 'to him', 'to her', 'to us', 'to them': indirect object pronouns

▶▶ **If you know what an indirect object pronoun is and how to use it, go on to 3.3.1.**

In English, an indirect object pronoun is the same as a direct object pronoun but has (or can have) 'to' or 'for' in front of it.

I bought her it. I bought it (direct object – it is the thing that you bought) for her (indirect object).

Give me it. Give it (direct object – the thing which is being given) to me (indirect object).

They showed him it. They showed it (direct object – the thing which is being shown) to him (indirect object).

Indirect pronouns are used with verbs like 'give/send/write/show/buy/offer/tell/lend' where you do something to/for someone/something.

I Identify the indirect object pronouns in these English sentences.

Try saying 'to/for' in front of the pronoun to see if it is indirect.

a Luigi sent me a text message.
b I could not read it. My friend can. I showed it her.
c She translated it for me.
d I wrote him a reply.
e She sent it for me.
f He sent her a new message.
g She did not show it me.
h She sent him a photo of herself.
i He sent her another message.
j She sent him a reply.
k She did not tell me what he said.
l She gave me my phone back and went.

3.3.1 *Mi, ti, gli, le*, etc.: indirect object pronouns

In Italian, you always put the indirect object pronoun in front of the verb except for *loro*, which goes after the verb.

Ti do 100 euro.	I am giving you 100 euros.
Mi ha detto che sono scemo!	S/He said (to) me that I was stupid!
Le ha fatto vedere la sua macchina nuova.	He showed (to) her his new car.
Non ci danno abbastanza soldi!	They don't give (to) us enough money!

Mi, ti, ci and *vi* are the same as the direct object pronouns, so you only have to remember:

Le ('to you', polite singular form, 'to him/her'),

gli/le ('to him/her'),

Loro ('to you' polite plural form, 'to them'),

and *gli/loro* ('to them').

II Fill in the missing pronouns.

a _____ ha dato la sua matita (to me)
b Chi _____ parla? (to us)
c Quanti soldi danno _____? (to them)
d _____ hai mandato il pacco? (to her)
e _____ ha parlato oggi? (to you, pl. fam.)
f Mia moglie _____ ha dato il biglietto? (to you, sing. fam.)
g _____ ha spiegato cosa devi fare? (to you, sing. fam.)
h _____ do un libro. (to her)
i Mio zio _____ ha dato una bottiglia di vino. (to him)
j _____ dai una mano? (to us)

3.3.2 The pronoun *ne*

Ne is used to replace *di* and a noun or pronoun. It is used
to mean 'of it' or 'of them', and has to be used in sentences
when it would be omitted in English:

Quante sorelle hai?   How many sisters have you got?
Ne ho tre.   I've got three (of them).

When used with a personal pronoun it will usually mean
something like 'of her/him/us' etc.

Mia madre è partita, e non   My mother has left, and I haven't
  ne ho notizie.   heard about her.
Conosci questi piloti? Sì, ne ho Do you know these racing
  spesso sentito parlare.   drivers? Yes, I have often
                                    heard of them.

3.3.3 Word order of pronouns: indirect + direct

▶▶ **If you don't want to know about this yet go on
to 3.4.**

If two or more pronouns are used together in a sentence,
they go in the order shown in the table below (this table
includes *si*, which is a reflexive pronoun). When *mi, ti, ci, vi*
and *si* precede another pronoun, they become *me, te, ce, ve*
and *se*. When *ne* is used it goes in the position indicated by
the final column of the table.

me lo	me la	me li	me le	me ne
te lo	te la	te li	te le	te ne
glielo	gliela	glieli	gliele	gliene
se lo	se la	se li	se le	se ne
ce lo	ce la	ce li	ce le	ce ne
ve lo	ve la	ve li	ve le	ve ne

III How would you say the following?

    a He gave it (m) to me.
    b I have written it to her.
    c She gave it (f) to them.
    d They gave it to you (sing).
    e You gave it to us.
    f She bought him it (m).
    g He read it to me.
    h He gave it to us.
    i We gave it to you (pl).
    j They read it to them.
    k She gave it (m) to me.
    l I won't give it (m) to you!

▶▶ **If you have had enough of pronouns move on to Chapter 4 and come back later.**

3.3.4 ▶Fast track: indirect object pronouns

In English, an indirect object pronoun is the same as a direct object pronoun but has (or can have) 'to' or 'for' in front of it.

Indirect pronouns are only used with verbs like: 'give/send/write/show/buy/offer/tell/lend' where you do something to/for someone.

In Italian, indirect object pronouns go in the same place as direct object pronouns. To sum up, this is:

- usually immediately in front of the verb, except *loro*, which always goes after;
- on the end of infinitives, imperatives, present participles, gerunds or *ecco*;
- compulsorily on the end of a positive command.

 The indirect object pronouns are very similar to the direct object pronouns.

mi	to me
ti	to you (familiar singular)
gli	to him
le	to her
gli/le	to it
Le	to you (formal singular)
ci	to us
vi	to you
gli/loro	to them
Loro	to you (formal plural)

If two or more pronouns are used together, they go in the following order:

me lo	me la	me li	me le	me ne
te lo	te la	te li	te le	te ne
glielo	gliela	glieli	gliele	gliene
se lo	se la	se li	se le	se ne
ce lo	ce la	ce li	ce le	ce ne
ve lo	ve la	ve li	ve le	ve ne

3.4 Me, te, lui, etc.: prepositional or disjunctive pronouns

Prepositional or disjunctive pronouns are only used when talking about people or animals. Most of them are the same as the subject pronouns.

> Con lui ('with him'), senza di lei ('without her'), di fronte a me ('in front of me'), per loro ('for them'), attorno a noi ('around us'), dietro di loro ('behind them'), etc.

Examples:

Questo libro è per te.	This book is for you.
Voglio andare a Roma con loro.	I want to go to Rome with them.
È per Lei?	Is it for you?
È con lei.	He's with her.
Compriamo un regalo per lui.	We're buying a present for him.
Andiamo con Loro?	Are we going with you?

Singular		**Plural**	
me	me	noi	us
te	you (familiar singular)	voi	you
lui	him/it	loro	them
lei	her/it		
sé	...self	sé	...selves
Lei	you (formal singular)	Loro	you (formal plural)

I Replace the people in italics with a pronoun.

a Questa macchina è di *Roberto*.
b Giovanni è andato in città con *sua moglie*.
c È uscita con *i suoi amici*.
d Il Signor Nosella ha comprato un regalo per *sua figlia*.

e La borsa blu è di *Riccardo*, e la borsa rossa è di *Isabella*.
f Ha mangiato con *i miei bambini e me*.
g È *sua madre*!
h Siamo partiti con *i nostri bambini*.
i Abbiamo comprato dei gelati per *te e per i tuoi amici*.
j Esco con *Gill*.

3.4.1 *Mi, ti, ci, vi, loro*, 'me', 'you', 'us', 'them' and the imperative

With imperatives, the words for 'me', 'you', 'us' and the reflexive pronouns are joined to the end of the imperative verb. The exception is *loro* ('to them'), which is never joined to the verb. After the imperatives *fa'*, *di'*, *da'*, *sta'* and *va'*, the initial consonant of the pronoun is doubled (e.g. *dimmi, dalla, fallo*).

II How would you say:

a Look at us!
b Give it to me!
c Do it!
d Wake up!
e Write it!

3.5 *Chi? Che/che cosa/cosa?*, 'Who?' 'What?': interrogative words

An interrogative word is used to ask questions like 'who', 'why', 'how', 'which'. Most are either pronouns or adverbs. Here are some common ones, with their meanings.

▶▶ **If you know all about interrogatives go on to 3.6.**

Chi?, 'who(m)?' This word means 'who' if it refers to the subject of the sentence and 'whom' if it refers to the object.

 Remember the subject is the person or thing who 'does' the action.

Chi è questa donna?	Who is this woman?
Con chi sei?	Who(m) are you with?

Di chi?, 'whose?' This word means 'whose' when it is used in a question clause.

Di chi è questa macchina?	Whose car is this?
Di chi è fratello?	Whose brother is he?

Che/che cosa/cosa?, 'what?' There are three ways of saying 'what?' in Italian – *che?*, *che cosa?* and just *cosa? Cosa* by itself is slightly more common in spoken Italian, but the others are used too.

Cos'è?	What is it?
Che cosa stai per mangiare?	What are you about to eat?
Cosa volete fare?	What would you like to do?

Quale? Quali?, 'which?' This word is used if there is a choice between two or more things. *Quale* is the singular and *quali* is the plural.

Ci sono due libri. Quale preferisci?	There are two books. Which do you prefer?
Ha tre sorelle. Quali sono qui?	He has three sisters. Which ones are here?

Quanto? quanta? quanti? quante?, 'how much?', 'how many?' Used as an adjective or a pronoun, this agrees with the nouns(s) it refers to. It is sometimes used as an adverb, in which case it doesn't change.

As an adjective or a pronoun:

Quanto vino hai?	How much wine have you got?
Quanto latte vuoi?	How much milk do you want?
Quanti fratelli hai?	How many brothers have you got?
Quante case ci sono nella città?	How many houses are there in the city?

As an adverb:

Quanto vale?	How much is it worth?

I Fill in the gaps in the following sentences:

a How much water do you want?   _____ acqua vuoi?
b How many sisters have you got?   _____ sorelle hai?
c Here are two rooms. Which do you prefer?   Ecco due camere. _____ preferisci?
d What would you like to drink?   _____ vuoi bere?
e Whose house is this?   _____ è questa casa?
f How much is this car worth?   _____ vale questa macchina?
g What do you like?   _____ ti piace?
h How many books have you got?   _____ libri hai?
i Which house is yours?   _____ casa è la tua?
j Who is this woman?   _____ è questa donna?

3.6 *Il mio, la mia, il tuo, la tua*: how to say 'it's mine', 'it's yours': possessive adjectives and pronouns

▶▶ **If you want to avoid using the possessives for the moment you can say instead *di Giovanni* etc. and go on to 3.7.**

mine	(il) mio	(la) mia	(i) miei	(le) mie
yours (informal sing.)	(il) tuo	(la) tua	(i) tuoi	(le) tue
his/hers/its	(il) suo	(la) sua	(i) suoi	(le) sue
yours (polite sing.)	(il) suo	(la) sua	(i) suoi	(le) sue
ours	(il) nostro	(la) nostra	(i) nostri	(le) nostre
yours (informal pl.)	(il) vostro	(la) vostra	(i) vostri	(le) vostre
theirs (masc. and fem.)	(il) loro	(la) loro	(i) loro	(le) loro
yours (polite pl.)	(il) loro	(la) loro	(i) loro	(le) loro

Possessive adjectives translate the English 'my', 'your', 'his/her/its', etc., and possessive pronouns are 'mine', 'yours', 'his', 'hers', 'ours', 'yours', 'theirs'. In Italian, possessive adjectives and pronouns are the same, and both are used with the definite article. They have to agree with the noun they are replacing. Remember to leave out the definite article with members of the family in the singular. This omission also applies after the verb *essere* in cases such as *Di chi è questa penna? – È mia/tua.*

Guardi questa macchina. È la mia.
(*la mia* to agree with *macchina*)

I Replace the nouns in italics with the correct form of the pronoun: (*il*) *mio*/(*la*) *mia*/(*le*) *mie*/(*i*) *miei*.

a Questo non è *il tuo libro*. È _____
b *Questa casa* appartiene a me. È _____
c Ecco *il vino* che ho comprato ieri. È _____
d Mi piace molto *la casa* dove abito. È _____
e Ci sono *una Lancia e una Fiat* nel garage. Sono _____
f Roberto e Paolo non sono *i tuoi fratelli*. Sono _____
g Maria e Assunta sono brave *sorelle*! Sono _____
h *Questi cani* non sono molto giovani. Sono _____

3.7 *Che, cui,* 'who', 'that', 'which': relative pronouns

How to express 'The one who, whom, which ...'

▶▶ **If you can recognise a relative pronoun, go on to 3.8.**

Relative pronouns are the words 'who', 'which', 'whom', 'that' and 'whose' when they are used to refer to someone already mentioned. Sometimes in English these words are completely missed out – but NEVER in Italian (e.g. 'the girl – I was with/the girl who/whom I was with'). Some of them look like question words, but they serve a different purpose – they link sentences, but they do not ask questions.

Che is the normal relative pronoun, but *cui* has to be used after a preposition.

la donna *che* abita a Roma	the woman *who* lives in Rome
il ragazzo *che* abbiamo visto in città	the boy (*whom*) we saw in town
il cane *che* abbaia ogni giorno	the dog *which/that* barks every day
la macchina *con cui* siamo arrivati	the car *in which* we arrived
il ragazzo *con cui* sono venuto	the boy *with whom* I came ('the boy I came with')
il paese *di cui* stavo parlando	the country (of which) I was talking

The part of the sentence after the relative pronoun is called a relative clause.

 A clause is a part of a sentence which doesn't make sense on its own but depends on the rest of the sentence to complete its meaning.

3.7.1 *Chi,* 'the person who'

You can use *chi* to say 'people who', 'the person who', 'he/she who', 'anyone who', etc., but even if the sense is plural the verb is always singular and any related adjective will be masculine.

Chi vuole uscire deve dirmelo ora.	(Anyone) who wants to leave must tell me now.
Chi non risparmia niente sarà povero.	(Those) who don't save anything will be poor.

3.7.2 *Quello che, quella che, ciò che,* 'that which', 'what'

Quello che and *ciò che* are used to translate 'what', meaning 'that which' (e.g. 'tell me about what you did today' = 'tell me about that which you did today'). These words are only used to give the meaning of 'what' when it isn't a question. Note also *quello/quella che* 'the one which' and *quelli/quelle che* 'the ones which'.

Quello che hai comprato non mi piace.	I don't like what you have bought.
Parliamo un po' di ciò che è successo.	Let's talk a bit about what happened.
Dammi la borsa, quella che è sul tavolo.	Give me the bag, the one which is on the table.

3.7.3 *Il quale/la quale/i quali/le quali,* 'the one(s) which'

Il quale/la quale/i quali/le quali is most commonly used after a preposition, and can be a direct replacement for *per cui, in cui,* etc.

la donna alla quale (a cui) ho spedito una cartolina	the woman to whom I have sent a postcard (the woman I have sent a postcard to)
le case nelle quali (in cui) abitavano	the houses in which they lived (the houses they lived in)
Ecco il ragazzo del quale (di cui) hai parlato.	There is the boy about whom you've talked. (the boy you've talked about)

3.7.4 *Il cui, la cui,* etc., 'whose'

Cui with a definite article (*il, la, i* or *le* only) has the meaning of 'whose'. The definite article has to agree in gender and number with the noun it refers to, but *cui* is invariable.

la macchina il cui motore è rumoroso	the car whose engine is noisy
il presidente il cui naso è grande	the president whose nose is big
le donne i cui bambini sono noiosi	the women whose children are boring
gli alberghi le cui camere sono care	the hotels whose rooms are expensive

I Complete the sentences using the appropriate relative pronoun form as best fits the meaning of the sentence:

a Come si chiama la ragazza ____ ho visto nel parco?	What's the name of the girl I saw in the park?
b Non conosco la signora ____ vive qui.	I don't know the woman who lives here.
c Non so ____ devo parlare di questo.	I don't know who to talk to about all this.
d Ecco il ragazzo ____ macchina mi ha colpito.	This is the boy whose car hit me.
e È una donna ____ non so niente.	She is a woman about whom I know nothing.
f Cerco un inglese ____ abita a Roma.	I'm looking for an Englishman who lives in Rome.

3.8 *Questo/questa, quello/quella*: 'this one', 'that one', etc.

There are two kinds of demonstrative pronoun in Italian which do the same job as 'this' and 'that' in English. They agree in number and gender with the noun they are referring to, and each has a different function according to how far the object being referred to is from the person who is speaking. When you would use 'this' in English (i.e. for something near you), use *questo/questa* (etc.). For something that is further away, use *quello/quella* (etc.). Here is a table of both words in all their forms.

Singular		Plural	
Masc.	**Fem.**	**Masc.**	**Fem.**
This (near you) questo	questa	questi	queste
That (further away) quello	quella	quelli	quelle

Quale degli anelli preferisci?	Which one of the rings do you prefer?
Preferisco questo.	I prefer this one (here).
Tu preferisci quello?	Do you prefer that one (there)?
Quali fiori preferisci?	Which flowers do you prefer?
Io preferisco questi e tu preferisci quelli.	I prefer these, and you prefer those.

I Say you want to order these things, using *questo/questa/ questi/queste.*

a un dolce [___]
b dei vermicelli [___]
c delle caramelle [___]
d una bottiglia di vino [___]
e un pacco di buste [___]
f una penna [___]
g un quadro [___]
h delle matite [___]
i delle scarpe bianche [___]
j dei guanti neri [___]

II Say you want those things, using *quello/quella/quelli/quelle.*

a una bottiglia di vino [___]
b dei libri [___]
c una macchina [___]
d dei guanti [___]
e delle tovaglie [___]
f un armadio marrone [___]
g delle tende [___]
h un televisore [___]
i un'autoradio [___]
j dei fiori [___]

3.9 ►Fast track: pronouns

A pronoun is a word which stands for a noun.

A Subject pronouns

A subject pronoun is a person or thing who does the action described by a verb: 'I' 'you' ... etc.

They can be used in front of verbs and to replace a person or thing already mentioned. In Italian they are usually missed out because the verb ending does their job (which is to show who or what the verb is referring to).

They are:

Singular		Plural	
io	I	noi	we
tu	you	voi	you
lui	he	loro	they
lei	she	Loro	you (formal)
Lei	you (formal)		

B   Direct object pronouns: 'me', 'you', etc.

The direct object pronoun stands in for the person or object who or which has the action done to it.

They are:

Singular		Plural	
mi	me	ci	us
ti	you	vi	you
lo	him/it	li	them (m)
la	her/it	le	them (f)
La	you (formal)	Li/Le	you (formal)

In English they come after the verb; in Italian they come in front of the verb except that they have to be attached to the end of infinitives, gerunds, imperatives and 'freestanding' past participles.

I see him ((I) him see)	Lo vedo
She sees me ((She) me sees)	Mi vede
They see you ((They) you see)	Ti vedono
We don't see them ((We) them don't see)	Non li vediamo

C   Indirect object pronouns: 'to me', 'to him', etc.

In English, an indirect object pronoun is the same as a direct object pronoun but has (or can have) 'to' or 'for' in front of it. In Italian there is a special set of them, most of which are very similar to the direct object pronouns.

Indirect object pronouns are normally placed in front of the verb, except that they have to be attached to the end of infinitives, gerunds, imperatives and 'freestanding' past participles.

They are:

Singular		Plural	
mi	to me	ci	to us
ti	to you (familiar)	vi	to you
gli	to him/it	gli/loro	to them
le	to her/it		
Le	to you (formal)	Loro	to you (formal)

Most indirect object pronouns are the same as the direct object pronouns.

If you have more than one pronoun in front of the verb, the pronouns go in the following order:

me lo	me la	me li	me le	me ne
te lo	te la	te li	te le	te ne
glielo	gliela	glieli	gliele	gliene
se lo	se la	se li	se le	se ne
ce lo	ce la	ce li	ce le	ce ne
ve lo	ve la	ve li	ve le	ve ne

 In the perfect tense the pronouns always come before the part of avere (except *loro*).

D   Disjunctive pronouns

There is a set of pronouns which are used after prepositions (e.g. *per me, con noi*) to provide emphasis etc. These are called disjunctive or emphatic pronouns.

Singular		**Plural**	
me	me	noi	us
te	you (familiar)	voi	you
lui/esso	him/it	loro/essi	them
lei/essa	her/it	loro/esse	them
sé	self	sé	selves
Lei	you (formal)	Loro	you (formal)

E   *Chi?, Che cosa?,* 'Who?', 'What?': interrogatives

These are used to ask questions like 'Who?' or 'What?'

Chi?, 'Who(m)?' This word means 'who' if it refers to the subject of the sentence and 'whom' if it refers to the object.

Di chi?, 'Whose?' This word means 'whose' when it is used in a question clause.

Che/che cosa/cosa?, 'What?' There are three ways of saying 'What?' in Italian: *Che?, Che cosa?,* and *just Cosa?.*

Quale? Quali?, 'Which?' This word is used if there is a choice between two or more things. *Quale?* is used when referring to singular objects or people, *Quali?* is used to refer to plurals.

Quanto? Quanta? Quanti? Quante?, 'How much?' 'How many?' Used as an adjective or a pronoun, it has to agree with the noun referred to: to ask how much use *Quanto? Quanta?* for how many use *Quanti? Quante?*

F *Il mio, la mia, il tuo, la tua,* etc.: possessive pronouns/adjectives

They translate the English 'my/mine', 'your(s)', 'his', 'her(s)', 'its', 'our(s)', 'your(s)', 'their(s)'. They have to agree with the noun they are replacing.

my/mine	(il) mio	(la) mia	(i) miei	(le) mie
your(s) (informal sg.)	(il) tuo	(la) tua	(i) tuoi	(le) tue
his/her(s)/its	(il) suo	(la) sua	(i) suoi	(le) sue
your(s) (polite sg.)	(il) suo	(la) sua	(i) suoi	(le) sue
our(s)	(il) nostro	(la) nostra	(i) nostri	(le) nostre
your(s) (informal pl.)	(il) vostro	(la) vostra	(i) vostri	(le) vostre
their(s) (masc. and fem.)	(il) loro	(la) loro	(i) loro	(le) loro
your(s) (polite pl.)	(il) loro	(la) loro	(i) loro	(le) loro

G *Che, cui,* etc., 'who', 'which', 'whose', etc.: relative pronouns

Che, cui, – 'who', 'that', 'whom', 'which'
Chi – 'the person who ...'
Quello che, quella che, ciò che – 'that which', 'what'
Il quale/la quale/i quali/le quali – 'the one(s) which'
Il cui, la cui, etc. – 'whose'

H *Questo/questa, quello/quella:* 'this', 'that', etc.

Singular		Plural	
Masc.	**Fem.**	**Masc.**	**Fem.**
questo	questa	questi	queste
quello	quella	quelli	quelle

4 ADJECTIVES

4.1 What is an adjective?

▶▶ **If you know what an adjective is, go on to 4.2.**

Adjectives are 'describing' words; you use them to say what something or someone is like.

I   Highlight the adjectives in these sentences.

   a Peter is short and fat.
   b She has long, blonde hair and green eyes.
   c He has just bought a new computer.
   d She likes to wear new clothes for parties and casual clothes for gardening.
   e Her car is large and old and has four-wheel drive.
   f Her boyfriend is tall and dark.
   g She manages a small insurance company.
   h He has an older sister and a younger brother.
   i Her favourite dish is spaghetti.
   j He likes his beer very cold.

4.1.1 Adjectival agreement

In Italian the adjective 'agrees' with the noun. Most singular adjectives end in -*o* when they are used with a masculine noun, and change their ending to -*a* with a feminine noun.

 There are some adjectives which don't work quite like this.

▶▶ **If you know about adjectival agreement, go on to 4.3.**

If the noun is masculine singular, the adjective usually ends in -*o*: *nuovo, vecchio.*

If the noun is feminine singular, the adjective usually ends in -*a*: *nuova, vecchia.*

If the noun is masculine plural, the adjective usually ends in -*i*: *nuovi, vecchi.*

If the noun is feminine plural, the adjective usually ends in -*e*: *nuove, vecchie.*

	Singular		Plural	
	Masc.	**Fem.**	**Masc.**	**Fem.**
new	nuovo	nuova	nuovi	nuove
old	vecchio	vecchia	vecchi	vecchie

II Fill in the right form of:

nuovo/nuova/nuovi/nuove or *vecchio/vecchia/vecchi/vecchie*
(your choice).

a un libro ____
b una casa ____
c negozi ____
d macchine ____
e un treno ____
f una televisione ____
g vestiti ____
h borsette ____

4.1.2 Regular adjectives

Most adjectives end in *-o* for the masculine, *-a* for the
feminine, *-i* for the masculine plural and *-e* for the feminine
plural. There are some exceptions, but these are usually
quite logical and easy to predict. Here are examples of the
main groups.

	Singular		Plural	
	Masc.	**Fem.**	**Masc.**	**Fem.**
new	nuovo	nuova	nuovi	nuove
little	piccolo	piccola	piccoli	piccole
good	buono	buona	buoni	buone
red	rosso	rossa	rossi	rosse

III Fill in the missing forms. Check your answers and work out
how the adjectives relate to each other and form a pattern.

	Singular		Plural	
	Masc.	**Fem.**	**Masc.**	**Fem.**
a happy				
b beautiful				
c ugly				
d tall				
e short				
f good				

	Singular		Plural	
	Masc.	**Fem.**	**Masc.**	**Fem.**
g bad **h** quiet **i** noisy **j** strange **k** shy **l** serious **m** frivolous **n** sensible **o** stupid **p** sincere **q** insincere **r** thin **s** fat **t** short (thing)				

4.1.3 Irregular adjectives

Most adjectives ending in -*e* don't change between the masculine and feminine singular and both the plural forms are the same as well – they both end in -*i*.

	Singular		Plural	
	Masc.	**Fem.**	**Masc.**	**Fem.**
green	verde	verde	verdi	verdi
strong	forte	forte	forti	forti

If an adjective ends in -*one* in the masculine singular, it changes the ending to -*ona* in the feminine, and to -*oni* and -*one* in the feminine and masculine plurals, like a regular adjective.

	Singular		Plural	
	Masc.	**Fem.**	**Masc.**	**Fem.**
talkative	chiacchierone	chiacchierona	chiacchieroni	chiacchierone

Some adjectives end in -*ista* in the masculine and feminine singular. These have a masculine plural ending in -*i* and a feminine plural ending in -*e*, as with regular adjectives.

	Singular		Plural	
	Masc.	**Fem.**	**Masc.**	**Fem.**
communist	comunista	comunista	comunisti	comuniste

Some adjectives do not change at all, in the feminine or masculine, or the singular or plural. The most common of these are colours.

	Singular		Plural	
	Masc.	**Fem.**	**Masc.**	**Fem.**
blue	blu	blu	blu	blu
brown	marrone	marrone	marrone	marrone
violet	viola	viola	viola	viola
pink	rosa	rosa	rosa	rosa

Adjectives ending in -*co* with the stress on the last syllable have to add an *h* before the -*i* or -*e* ending in the masculine and feminine plural (to keep the *c* sound hard, like *k* in English).

	Masc.	**Fem.**	**Masc.**	**Fem.**
little (not much)	poco	poca	pochi	poche

Most adjectives ending in -*co* form their masculine plural by simply adding -*i* (so the *c* sound is softened, to sound like 'ch' in English), but keep the *h* in the feminine (so the *c* stays hard).

	Masc.	**Fem.**	**Masc.**	**Fem.**
public	pubblico	pubblica	pubblici	pubbliche

All adjectives ending in -*go* add an *h* in the plural before the -*i* or -*e* (as with the adjectives ending in -*co*, this is to stop the *g* sound being softened to an English *j* sound by the *i* and the *e*).

Singular		Plural	
Masc.	**Fem.**	**Masc.**	**Fem.**
lungo	lunga	lunghi	lunghe

Adjectives with an *i* in penultimate place don't add another *i* in the masculine plural but are otherwise regular:

	Singular		Plural	
	Masc.	**Fem.**	**Masc.**	**Fem.**
contrary	contrario	contraria	contrari	contrarie

A small number of adjectives ending in a consonant followed by *-cio* or *-gio* lose the *i* in the plural form (because it would be hard to say, and the *i* and *e* that follow do its job anyway):

	Singular		Plural	
	Masc.	**Fem.**	**Masc.**	**Fem.**
smooth	liscio	liscia	lisci	lisce
wise	saggio	saggia	saggi	sagge

The adjectives *buono* and *buona* change in the singular only when they are before a noun, and when the noun begins with a vowel; used without a noun the masculine singular is *buono*.

	Singular		Plural		
	Masc.	**Masc. + vowel**	**Fem.**	**Masc.**	**Fem.**
good	buon	buono + consonant	buona buon' + vowel	buoni	buone

The adjective *grande* changes in the singular only in the following ways:

	Singular		Plural	
	Masc. and fem.	**Masc. and fem.**	**Masc. and fem.**	**Masc. and fem.**
	+ consonant	**+ z/gn/ps/x**	**+ vowel**	
large	gran	grande	grand'	grandi

The adjective *bello* changes like the definite article and the demonstrative adjective *quello*, according to what follows it:

	Singular					Plural		
Masc.			**Fem.**			**Masc.**		**Fem.**
Before a conso-nant	Before s with a conso-nant	Before a vowel	Before a conso-nant	Before a vowel		Before a conso-nant	Before s conso-nant/ before vowel	Before any-thing
bel quel	bello quello	bell' quell'	bella quella	bell' quell'		bei quei	begli quegli	belle quelle

IV   Choose the right form of the adjective in brackets.

a   Il Signor Barlaam è _____ (comunista).
b   La Signora Barlaam è molto _____ (chiacchierone).
c   I maglioni sono _____ (viola).
d   Le pelli sono molto _____ (liscio).
e   Abbiamo _____ (poco) soldi. Siamo molto _____ (povero).
f   Il cielo è _____ (blu).
g   Questi cani sono _____ (marrone).
h   Gli spaghetti sono _____ (lungo).
i   C'è _____ (poco) gente qui, oggi.
j   Abbiamo delle _____ (bello) mele.
k   Vini _____ (forte) in vendita qui.
l   Ci sono dei _____ (bello) gnocchi in questo negozio.
m   Dove sono i gabinetti _____ (pubblico), per favore?
n   Quand'è il _____ (Grande) Premio d'Italia?
o   A Venezia ci sono dei canali _____ (grande).
p   _____ (Buono) viaggio!
q   La casa è molto _____ (grande).
r   I miei fratelli sono molto _____ (chiacchierone).
s   Questi uomini sono molto _____ (forte).
t   I miei genitori sono molto _____ (saggio).

4.1.4   Adjectives of nationality

Most adjectives of nationality end in an *-o* or an *-e*. Those ending in an *-o* in the masculine have a final *-a* for the feminine form. Those ending in an *-e* stay the same in the feminine form.

	Singular		Plural	
	Masc.	**Fem.**	**Masc.**	**Fem.**
Belgian	belga	belga	belgi	belghe*
Moroccan	marocchino	marocchina	marocchini	marocchine
German	tedesco	tedesca	tedeschi	tedesche
American	americano	americana	americani	americane

	Singular		Plural	
	Masc.	**Fem.**	**Masc.**	**Fem.**
French	francese	francese	francesi	francesi
English	inglese	inglese	inglesi	inglesi
Canadian	canadese	canadese	canadesi	canadesi
Scottish	scozzese	scozzese	scozzesi	scozzesi
Spanish	spagnolo	spagnola	spagnoli	spagnole
Italian	italiano	italiana	italiani	italiane
Swiss	svizzero	svizzera	svizzeri	svizzere
Russian	russo	russa	russi	russe

* This is irregular!

V Fill in the nationalities in the correct form.

    a Michael Schumacher è _____.
    b Jensen Button è _____.
    c Madonna è _____.
    d Luciano Pavarotti è _____.
    e Plácido Domingo e José Carreras sono _____.
    f Tim Henman e Kelly Holmes sono _____.
    g Roger Federer è _____.
    h Tom e Martha abitano a Washington: sono _____.
    i Billy Connolly è _____.
    j Questi signori vengono da Montreal: sono _____.

4.1.5 Colours

Most adjectives of colour agree in the same way as other adjectives, and they always come after the noun they describe: a red train becomes a train red, *un treno rosso*; the White House becomes the house white, *la Casa Bianca*.

Choose a phrase to memorise to help you remember the order: *un vino bianco, un gatto nero*, etc.

Don't forget that the adjectives come after the noun they are with, and that they 'agree' in gender and number with the noun.

The adjectives of colour form their agreements using the same rules as the other adjectives.

Note that some of the colours (e.g. *rosa, viola*) are invariable, i.e. don't change for masculine/feminine and plurals; *verde* only has the one singular form and the one plural form.

	Singular		Plural	
	Masc.	**Fem.**	**Masc.**	**Fem.**
red	rosso	rossa	rossi	rosse
yellow	giallo	gialla	gialli	gialle
blue	azzurro	azzurra	azzurri	azzurre
	blu	blu	blu	blu
green	verde	verde	verdi	verdi
black	nero	nera	neri	nere
white	bianco	bianca	bianchi	bianche
grey	grigio	grigia	grigi	grigie
brown	marrone	marrone	marrone	marrone
orange	arancione	arancione	arancioni	arancioni
purple	viola	viola	viola	viola
pink	rosa	rosa	rosa	rosa

VI Complete the sentences with the right form of the colour given in brackets.

a Alessandra porta una camicia _____ (rosso).
b I suoi guanti sono _____ (marrone).
c Il medico porta una camicia _____ (verde).
d Il suo impermeabile è _____ (azzurro).
e Maria porta un vestito _____ (arancione).
f Le sue scarpe sono _____ (bianco).
g Carlo indossa un maglione _____ (viola).
h I suoi guanti sono _____ (giallo).
i Enrico porta una cintura _____ (nero).
j I suoi stivali sono _____ (grigio).
k Le loro sciarpe sono _____ (rosa).

4.2 The position of adjectives

In English, adjectives come in front of the noun they are describing: 'a large house', 'a fast car'. In Italian most adjectives come after the noun ('a house large', 'a car fast'). A few adjectives can come before the noun:

bello	beautiful	grande	big, large
buono	good	grosso	big, large
breve	short	largo	wide
brutto	bad, ugly	lungo	long
cattivo	bad	piccolo	small
giovane	young	vecchio	old

Some change their meaning according to whether they come before or after the noun:

Adjective	Meaning before noun	Meaning after noun
alto	high	tall
basso	low	small, low (number)
buono	good (in ability)	good (in quality)
caro	dear, precious	dear, expensive
cattivo	bad, unpleasant	bad, evil
certo	(a) certain, some	certain, reliable
diverso	various, several	different
dolce	good, sweet	fresh (water)
grande	great	big, tall
grosso	big, serious (thing)	big, well built (person)
nuovo	new (another one)	new (i.e. not old)
numeroso	numerous, many	large in number
povero	poor, unfortunate	poor (i.e. not rich)
santo	blessed (expletive)	holy ('sainted')
semplice	just, simply, only	simple, easy
unico	(only) one	unique, special
vario	various, several	different
vero	real (emphatic)	true, authentic

alta stagione	high season
un uomo alto	a tall man
una povera donna	a poor (unfortunate) woman
una donna povera	a poor (impoverished) woman

4.3 ▶Fast track: adjectives

1 Most adjectives end in -o and -a in the singular and -i and -e in the plural.

2 Most adjectives ending in -e don't change in the singular. The plural forms end in -i.

3 Adjectives ending in -one and -ona in the singular change to -oni and -one in the plural.

4 Adjectives ending in -ista in both singular forms make their plurals with -isti and -iste.

5 Some adjectives do not change at all, in the feminine or masculine, or the singular or plural.

6 Adjectives ending in -co with the stress on the penultimate syllable add an h before the ending in the plural.

7 Adjectives ending in -co form their masculine plural by adding -i, but also add an h in the feminine plural.

8 Adjectives ending in -go add an h in the plural before the -i or -e.

9 Adjectives with an *i* in penultimate place don't add another *i* in the masculine plural.
10 Adjectives ending in a consonant followed by *-cio* or *-gio* lose the *i* in the plural form.
11 *Buono* changes in the singular before a noun, and when the noun begins with a vowel.
12 *Grande* changes in the singular only (see table above).
13 *Bello* changes in the singular and the plural (see table above).
14 Most adjectives of nationality end in *-e* in the masculine and the feminine singular, or in *-o* in the masculine and *-a* in the feminine singular, and they end in *-i*, or in *-i* and *-e* respectively, in the plural.

Singular		Plural	
Masc.	**Fem.**	**Masc.**	**Fem.**
1 un maglione rosso	una camicia rossa	maglioni rossi	camicie rosse
2 un treno verde	una macchina verde	treni verdi	macchine verdi
3 un uomo chiacchierone	una donna chiacchierona	uomini chiacchieroni	donne chiacchierone
4 un uomo comunista	una donna comunista	uomini comunisti	donne comuniste
5 un libro blu	una borsetta blu	libri blu	borsette blu
6 poco vino	poca acqua	pochi vini	poche acque
7 un gabinetto pubblico	una legge pubblica	gabinetti pubblici	leggi pubbliche
8 un pasto lungo	una bibita lunga	pasti lunghi	bibite lunghe
9 il senso contrario	la direzione contraria	i sensi contrari	le direzioni contrarie
10 un padre saggio	una madre saggia	padri saggi	madri sagge
11 buon giorno!	buona notte!	buoni giorni	buone notti
12 Il Gran Premio	la casa grande	i grandi premi	le case grandi
13 un bel canto	una bella ragazza	dei begli spaghetti	delle belle case
14 un uomo tedesco	una donna tedesca	uomini tedeschi	donne tedesche

A Word order

Most adjectives come after the word they are describing:

una macchina rossa — a red car; un uomo bravo — a good man; una ragazza giovane — a young girl

but these ones often come in front:

bello, buono, breve, brutto, cattivo, giovane, grande, grosso, largo, lungo, piccolo, vecchio

B   Adjectives with more than one meaning

Some adjectives change their meaning according to
whether they come before or after the noun:

> una nuova macchina – a new car (i.e. a different one); una
> macchina nuova – a new car (i.e. not a used one)

C   Colours

Like most other adjectives, the adjectives of colour come
after the word they are describing.

> un cane nero – a black dog

Most colours take the same endings as other adjectives:

> rosso, rossa, rossi, rosse

4.4   Comparative and superlative

The comparative is the form you use when you are
comparing two things and say, for example, that something
is bigger, smaller, newer, older, etc.

The superlative is the form when you say something is the
best, biggest, smallest, best of all.

Adjective	Comparative	Superlative

big
una macchina
  grande
	bigger
	una macchina più
	  grande
		biggest
		la macchina
		  più grande

small
una macchina
  piccola
	smaller
	una macchina più
	  piccola
		smallest
		la macchina
		  più piccola

 As *grande* and *piccolo* are adjectives they still have to agree with
the noun they describe.

4.4.1   Comparing two people or things

In Italian, you put *più* ('more') in front of the adjective. For
'than' you use *di* before names, pronouns, numerals and
adverbs. Before adverbs, nouns, pronouns, participles,
infinitives, prepositional phrases which are dependent on
the same verb, and between two adjectives, you use *che* to
translate 'than'.

Il Signor Barlaam è importante, ma la Signora Barlaam è più importante.	Mr Barlaam is important but Mrs Barlaam is more important.
Luigi è piccolo, ma sua sorella è più piccola.	Luigi is small but his sister is smaller.
Riccardo è intelligente, ma suo fratello è più intelligente di lui.	Riccardo is intelligent but his brother is more intelligent than him.
Viaggio più con la macchina che col treno.	I travel more by car than by train.

I Say the second things are all 'more' than the first:

a Questa macchina è veloce, ma quella è _____

b Tua sorella è bella, ma mia sorella è _____

c I nostri cani sono grandi, ma i vostri sono _____

d I libri di Giulio Cesare sono interessanti, ma quelli di Dante Alighieri sono _____

e L'esame d'italiano è difficile, ma quello di matematica è _____

f La Francia è un bel paese, ma l'Italia è un paese _____

g Questa casa è molto cara, ma quella è _____

h I miei genitori sono poveri, ma i tuoi sono _____

i Stai per comprare una radio cara, ma stiamo per comprare una radio _____

j Questa bicicletta è molto bella, ma cerchiamo una bicicletta _____ per nostro figlio.

To say something is less you use *meno* instead of *più*:

Alessandro è meno vecchio di suo fratello.	Alexander is less old than his brother.

II Say these things are all 'more' or 'less' than ...

a (+) La Ferrari è _____ veloce della McLaren.

b (+) Una Lancia è _____ cara di una Fiat.

c (−) Luigi è _____ intelligente di sua sorella.

d (+) Il serpente è _____ pericoloso dello scorpione.

e (+) Il cane è _____ grande del gatto.

f (−) Le Dolomiti sono _____ alte degli Appennini.

g (−) La Sardegna è _____ grande della Sicilia.

h (+) Torino si trova _____ a nord di Roma.

i (−) L'argento è _____ prezioso dell'oro.

j (+) Il presidente Silvio Berlusconi è _____ famoso del Senatore Giovanni Agnelli.

4.4.2 The superlative

il/la/i/le ... più ...

il/la/i/le ... meno ...

To say 'the most' and 'the least' you use *più* and *meno*. The adjective has to agree with the noun in gender and number, as usual, and you don't repeat the determiner:

la casa meno piccola
il cane più stupido

Even when the adjective follows the noun you don't repeat the determiner:

È il vino più caro della cantina.	It's the most expensive wine in the winery.
Ecco il gatto più bello del negozio.	It's the most beautiful cat in the shop.

III Fill in these comparisons.

a (+) Venezia è la città ____ bella del mondo.
b (+) La Rolls-Royce è la macchina ____ cara del mondo.
c (+) La balena è il mammifero ____ grande di tutti i mammiferi.
d (+) La zanzara è l'insetto ____ pericoloso di tutti.
e (–) La Città del Vaticano è il paese ____ grande del mondo.
f (–) Il chihuahua è il cane ____ grande del mondo.

4.4.3 Saying 'as (big) as'

If you are comparing two things which are similar, you use the expressions *tanto ... quanto* or *così ... come* ('as (big) as'). As with other comparatives, the adjectives have to agree with the noun they are describing.

È (tanto) alto quanto suo padre.	He is as tall as his father.
Questo vino è (così) buono come quello.	This wine is as good as that (one).

IV Say these places are (1) bigger; (2) less big; (3) as big as ... Remember to make the adjective agree with the noun where necessary.

a L'Albergo Intercontinentale è _____ l'Albergo Reale. (3)
b La città di Roma è _____ città di Milano. (1)
c Il porto di Marghera è _____ porto di Napoli. (2)
d Gli ipermercati *Carrefour* sono _____ supermercati *Penny*. (1)
e La Lombardia è _____ Liguria. (1)

4.4.4 Irregular comparitives

The words for 'better', 'worse', 'bigger' and 'smaller' have optional irregular forms which do not form their comparative with *più* or *meno*. Unlike the other adjective comparative words, these four words are invariable in the singular and do not have to agree with the noun they are describing.

più buono or migliore	better
più cattivo or peggiore	worse
più grande or maggiore	bigger (used for people, implying older)
più piccolo or minore	smaller (used for people, implying younger)

These adjectives are the same in masculine and feminine singular forms: *migliore, peggiore, maggiore, minore*. The masculine and feminine plural forms are: *migliori, peggiori, maggiori* and *minori*.

As with the other comparisons, 'than' is expressed by *di*, and it is just omitted if there is no follow-up to the comparison (in other words if only one thing is said to be better, worse, etc.).

Giovanni è il fratello minore di Giulio.
Il formaggio francese è buono ma quello italiano è migliore.

V   Insert the Italian for the word in brackets:

a Questo vino è buono, ma l'altro è (better).
b I miei voti sono (worse) dell'anno scorso!
c Franco è (older) di Rosario.
d Rosaria è (younger) di Palma.
e Rosario e Rosaria sono (younger) di Franco e Palma.
f I calciatori dell'Inter sono (better) dei calciatori del Milan.

4.5   ▶Fast track: comparative and superlative

A   The comparative

This is the form you use when you are comparing two things and say, for example, that something is bigger, smaller, newer or older.

In English we can either add '-er' or use the word 'more':

green	greener or more green
healthy	healthier or more healthy
tired	tireder or more tired

In Italian there is only one way. You add the word *più* (more) or *meno* (less).

più verde; più intelligente; meno stanco

As the word is an adjective it still must agree with the noun.

L'albero è più verde.	The tree is greener.
È meno stanca di me.	She is less tired than me.

B   The Superlative
When you are talking about the best or the worst you use
the superlative. In Italian the superlative is made by
inserting *il, la, i* or *le* before the *più* or *meno*. Note, however,
that when the adjective follows the noun, as most do, the
article is not repeated, since it goes in its normal place
before the noun. e.g.

la studentessa più intelligente   the most intelligent student in
   della classe   the class
i biglietti meno cari di tutti   the cheapest tickets of all

As the word is an adjective it still must agree with the noun:

il bambino più terribile
la ragazza più bella
i libri più interessanti

C   'Better', 'worse', 'older' and 'younger'
The optional words for 'better', 'worse', 'older' and
'younger' (*migliore/i, peggiore/i, maggiore/i and minore/i*) do
not change for masculine/feminine, only for singular/
plural.

più buono **or** migliore   better
più cattivo **or** peggiore   worse
più grande **or** maggiore   bigger (used for people,
                                                implying older)
più piccolo **or** minore   smaller (used for people,
                                                implying younger)

Di or *che* are omitted if there is no follow-up to the
comparison.

Il formaggio francese è buono ma quello italiano è migliore.

5 ADVERBS

What is an adverb?

Adverbs are words which describe a verb.

She drives *fast*. He speaks *too loudly*.

Some adverbs can qualify an adjective or adverb, e.g. 'very' ('fast'), 'quite' ('loud'), 'too' ('hard').

5.1 Formation of adverbs

5.1.1 Regular adverbs

Most Italian adverbs are formed by adding -*mente* to the feminine singular form of the adjective, if this is different from the masculine singular:

lento/lenta > lentamente	slowly
rapido/rapida > rapidamente	quickly
alto/alta > altamente	loudly

Adjectives which already end in -*e* just need to add -*mente* after it:

dolce > dolcemente	gently
recente > recentemente	recently

Adjectives which end in -*le* or -*re* lose the final -*e* and add -*mente*:

facile > facilmente	easily
regolare > regolarmente	regularly

When the -*le* or -*re* have another consonant before, the *e* is retained and -*mente* is added:

folle > follemente	madly
mediocre > mediocremente	poorly

Altrimenti (differently, otherwise) is just… different. And so is *violentemente*.

5.1.2 Irregular adverbs

Some adverbs are irregular and are not like their adjectives:

buono – good (adj.)	bene – well (adverb)
migliore – better	meglio – better
cattivo – bad	male – badly
peggiore – worse	peggio – worse

I Make these adjectives into adverbs:

a secco
b folle
c semplice
d rapido
e facile
f regolare
g raro
h cattivo
i vero
j buono

5.1.3 Adverbs to watch

Here are some adverbs of degree – these can qualify other adverbs or adjectives and are often used with them:

meno	less
poco	not very, little
abbastanza	quite
così	so much
tanto	so, so much, so very
molto	very
più	more
troppo	too (much)

These are adverbs of time and frequency:

adesso/ora	now
allora	then
ancora	yet
dopo	after
già	already
ormai	by now
poi	then
presto	soon, quickly, fast
subito	immediately
mai	never
sempre	always
spesso	often

5.2 ▶Fast track: adverbs

Adverbs are words which describe an action: 'well', 'fast', 'slowly' etc.

In English most words which end in -'ly' are adverbs: 'naturally', 'romantically', 'sadly' etc.

In Italian most adverbs are made by adding -*mente* to the feminine singular form of the adjective, if it is different from the masculine:

lento/lenta	lentamente
sicuro/sicura	sicuramente
dolce	dolcemente
regolare	regolarmente

Some useful adverbs:

bene	well
male	badly
poco	little
meglio	better
spesso	frequently/often

These words are used with another adverb or adjective:

molto – molto piccolo	very small
poco – poco bello	not very beautiful
sempre – sempre guasto	always out of order
qualche volta – qualche volta felice	sometimes happy
abbastanza – abbastanza brutto	quite ugly
troppo – troppo caro	too expensive

6 PREPOSITIONS

6.1 Recognising prepositions

▶▶ **If you know what a preposition is go on to 6.2**

Prepositions are words like 'in', 'on', and 'under'. Unlike adjectives, they do not change. They are usually used in conjunction with a noun or pronoun, e.g. 'in the cupboard', 'near the station', 'for her', 'with me'.

Prepositions can tell you:

where a person or thing is, i.e. its position:

sotto la tavola	under the table
dentro la casa	inside the house

how something is done, i.e. manner:

con burro	with butter
senz'acqua	without water

when something happens, i.e. time:

fra cinque minuti	in five minutes
dopo cena	after dinner

for whom something is done:

per me	for me

6.2 Some common prepositions

The following section looks at the most common prepositions.

6.2.1 A, da, di, in and su

These prepositions change when they are used with the definite article, and combine to form a separate set of words (in the same way as the adjective *bello* does). They have a set of forms which correspond to *il, la* etc. depending on the first letter(s) of the following noun. One or two other prepositions such as *con* also have similar sets of forms, but they are not often used. Here is a table of how the changes work:

Prep.	Before il	Before la	Before l'	Before lo	Before i	Before le	Before gli	
a	al	alla	all'	allo	ai	alle	agli	to/at/in/on the
da	dal	dalla	dall'	dallo	dai	dalle	dagli	from the
di	del	della	dell'	dello	dei	delle	degli	of the
in	nel	nella	nell'	nello	nei	nelle	negli	in/to the
su	sul	sulla	sull'	sullo	sui	sulle	sugli	on the

A (or *al, dal,* etc.) can mean 'to', 'at', 'in', 'of' or 'on', according to the context:

Siamo a casa.	We are at home.
Arriviamo alle (= a le) dieci.	We arrive at ten.
Abito a Venezia.	I live in Venice.
Oggi vado a Roma.	Today I am going to Rome.
Andiamo a cavallo.	Let's go on horseback.
un panino al formaggio	a cheese sandwich

A is used with names of towns and cities but not for countries or regions.

Da is usually used to say where something or someone is from:

Vengo da Treviso.	I come from Treviso.
Stava uscendo dal (= da il) negozio.	He was coming from/out of the shop.

It can also signify something's purpose, or what it is for:

la stanza da bagno	bathroom (= room for bath)
una tazza da tè	a teacup (= cup for tea)

Note: una tazza di tè – a cup of tea

Sometimes it is used after adverbs to complement an infinitive, with the meaning 'to':

Non c'è niente da fare.	There's nothing to do.

It can also mean 'for': *Studio l'italiano da tre anni.*

Or 'to': *Vado dal dentista.*

Or 'by': *È stato scritto da Paolo.*

Di usually has the sense of 'of', and is used in Italian (and other southern European languages) instead of the Saxon genitive ('s) which is commonly used in English and

German – in other words, you don't say 'Francesco's dog', but 'the dog of (*di*) Francesco':

la macchina di Roberto	Robert's car (= the car of Roberto)
la casa di mia madre	my mother's house (= the house of my mother)
la sorella di Ermenegildo	Ermenegildo's sister (= the sister of Ermenegildo)
una vista del (= di il) mare	a view of the sea
una bottiglia di vino	a bottle of wine
una tazza di tè (see above under da)	a cup of tea
una bottiglia di acqua minerale frizzante	a bottle of fizzy mineral water

In can mean 'to', 'in' or 'by', according to the context:

Andiamo in città.	Let's go to (= into) town.
Vado in Scozia.	I'm going to Scotland.
Mia madre aspetta in giardino.	My mother is waiting in the garden.
Andiamo in treno.	We're going by train.
Capodanno è in gennaio.	New Year's Day is in January.

In is used rather than *a* with names of countries and regions, and is often used for other places (*sono/vado in montagno/in spiaggia* etc.).

Su is usually used to show something's position at or on a place or thing, and it can have the sense of 'about', as in English (e.g. 'a book on cooking'). It can also mean 'out of' as in a fraction ('8 out of 10', or '8 over 10').

La tua maglia è sulla tavola.	Your sweater is on the table.
Questo è un libro sul Rinascimento italiano.	This is a book on (= about) the Italian Renaissance.
Hai ottenuto otto su dieci.	You got eight out of ten.

6.2.2 *Per*

Per usually means the same as 'for' or 'in the direction of'. It can also mean 'through'.

Ecco un regalo per te.	Here is a present for you.
Il treno per Venezia parte alle dieci.	The train for Venice leaves at 10.
Passa per Brescia alle sette.	It goes through Brescia at 7.
Chiamo per telefono.	I'm calling by phone.

6.2.3 *Con*

Con usually means the same as 'with'. It can also mean 'on', when it is used with a means of transport.

Mia madre viene sempre con me.	My mother always comes with me.
chilli con carne	chilli with meat
Guidate con prudenza.	Drive carefully (= with prudence).
Sono venuto con il treno delle 8.	I came on the 8 o'clock train.

6.2.4 *Fra*

Fra means the same as 'in' used with time (e.g. 'in five minutes', 'in three hours'), or it can have the sense of 'among' or 'between':

Torno fra cinque minuti.	I'll be back in five minutes.
Ci vediamo fra poco.	We'll see each other in a little while.
Il villaggio si trova fra i monti.	The village is (situated) in the mountains.

6.2.5 *Tra*

Tra usually means the same as *between* or *among* and is used with expressions of space.

La casa si trova tra i due negozi.	The house is between the two shops.
Un cane è tra gli agnelli.	A dog is among the lambs.
L'abbiamo discusso tra di noi.	We discussed it amongst ourselves.
Alcune tra queste donne sono inglesi.	Some of these women are English.

6.2.6 *Sopra* and *sotto*

Sopra usually means the same as 'above'. *Sotto* means the same as 'under'.

Il baldacchino è sopra il letto.	The canopy is above the bed.
Il gabinetto è sopra la cucina.	The toilet is above the kitchen.
Siamo seduti sotto l'albero.	We are sitting under the tree.
Ha parlato sotto voce.	He spoke in a low voice ('under voice').

I How would you say you were going to these places?

Vado ...

a la spiaggia
b l'albergo
c la piscina
d l'ospedale
e il museo
f la discoteca

g il teatro
h la stazione ferroviaria
i la banca
j il distributore (petrol station)

*With some of these words *in* can be used instead of *a*.

II Say what these things are made of or who they belong to by
putting in the appropriate preposition, combining it with
the definite article as necessary.

a a ham sandwich	un panino _____ prosciutto
b a vanilla ice cream	un gelato _____ vaniglia
c the girls' books	i libri _____ ragazze
d the teacher's car	la macchina _____ professore
e the windscreen of the car	il parabrezza _____ macchina
f a cup of coffee	una tazza _____ caffè
g a bottle of (the) red wine	una bottiglia _____ vino rosso
h the friends' garden	il giardino _____ amici
i my mother's book	il libro _____ mia madre
j a cheese pizza	una pizza _____ formaggio

III Complete these sentences with the correct prepositions.

a Ieri sera sono andato _____ Venezia _____ il mio amico.	Last night I went to Venice with my friend.
b Abbiamo passato un paio di ore _____ bar.	We spent a couple of hours in the bar.
c Là, abbiamo parlato _____ due belle ragazze.	There we chatted to two pretty girls.
d Poi abbiamo preso il treno insieme _____ Mestre.	Then we took the train together to Mestre.
e Da Mestre siamo andati _____ il bus _____ Padova.	From Mestre we went by bus to Padua.
f A Padova siamo andati _____ discoteca.	In Padua we went to the disco.
g Le due ragazze hanno ballato _____ noi.	The two girls danced with us.
h La discoteca si trova _____ la stazione.	The discotheque is above the station.

6.3 ▶Fast track: prepositions

Prepositions are words like 'in', 'on' and 'under'. They do
not change. They tell you:

where a person or thing is, i.e. its position
how something is done, i.e. manner

Regular verbs

	Present indicative	Present subjunctive	Present participle	Gerund	Imperative	Future	Conditional	Imperfect	Perfect	Past definite
-are verbs **parlare** to speak, talk	parlo	parli	parlante	parlando		parlerò	parlerei	parlavo	ho parlato	parlai
	parli	parli			parla	parlerai	parleresti	parlavi	hai parlato	parlasti
	parla	parli			parli	parlerà	parlerebbe	parlava	ha parlato	parlò
	parliamo	parliamo			parliamo	parleremo	parleremmo	parlavamo	abbiamo parlato	parlammo
	parlate	parliate			parlate	parlerete	parlereste	parlavate	avete parlato	parlaste
	parlano	parlino			parlino	parleranno	parlerebbero	parlavano	hanno parlato	parlarono
-ere verbs **vendere** to sell	vendo	venda	vendente	vendendo		venderò	venderei	vendevo	ho venduto	vendei
	vendi	venda			vendi	venderai	venderesti	vendevi	hai venduto	vendesti *
	vende	venda			venda	venderà	venderebbe	vendeva	ha venduto	vendé **
	vendiamo	vendiamo			vendiamo	venderemo	venderemmo	vendevamo	abbiamo venduto	vendemmo
	vendete	vendiate			vendete	venderete	vendereste	vendevate	avete venduto	vendeste ***
	vendono	vendano			vendano	venderanno	venderebbero	vendevano	hanno venduto	venderono

*vendetti
**vendette
***vendettero

*These are alternative regular forms.

Verb Tables

	Present indicative	Present subjunctive	Present participle	Gerund	Imperative	Future	Conditional	Imperfect	Perfect	Past definite
-ire verbs **servire** to serve	servo	serva	servente	servendo		servirò	servirei	servivo	ho servito	servii
	servi	serva			servi	servirai	serviresti	servivi	hai servito	servisti
	serve	serva			serva	servirà	servirebbe	serviva	ha servito	servì
	serviamo	serviamo			serviamo	serviremo	serviremmo	servivamo	abbiamo servito	servimmo
	servite	serviate			servite	servirete	servireste	servivate	avete servito	serviste
	servono	servano			servano	serviranno	servirebbero	servivano	hanno servito	servirono
-ire verbs **finire*** to finish	finisco	finisca								
	finisci	finisca			finisci					
	finisce	finisca			finisca					
	finiamo	finiamo			finiamo					
	finite	finiate			finite					
	finiscono	finiscano			finiscano					

*Other verbs of this type are: *abolire, capire, colpire, condire, contribuire, costruire, digerire, diminuire, distribuire, fallire, favorire, garantire, gradire, impazzire, impedire, inserire, istruire, patire, preferire, proibire, pulire, punire, reagire, restituire, riunire, sostituire, sparire, spedire, stabilire, stupire, suggerire, trasferire, ubbidire, unire.*

Otherwise regular -are verbs with spelling adjustments

a) Verbs in -care and -gare

	Present indicative	Present subjunctive	Present participle	Gerund	Imperative	Future	Conditional	Imperfect	Perfect	Past definite
cercare to look for, try	cerco cerchi cerca cerchiamo cercate cercano	cerchi cerchi cerchi cerchiamo cerchiate cerchino			cerca cerchi cerchiamo cercate cerchino	cercherò	cercherei			
pagare to pay	pago paghi paga paghiamo pagate pagano	paghi paghi paghi paghiamo paghiate paghino			paga paghi paghiamo pagate paghino	pagherò	pagherei			

Note that the *h* is retained throughout the future and conditional.

b) Verbs in -iare

Verbs ending in *-iare* with an unstressed *i*, for example *studiare*, have only one *i* in the forms referred to below, not the double *i* you would expect.

	Present indicative	Present subjunctive	Present participle	Gerund	Imperative	Future	Conditional	Imperfect	Perfect	Past definite
studiare to study, learn	(tu) studi (noi) studiamo	studi studi studi studiamo studiate studino			studi (Lei) studiamo studino					

Note that verbs ending in *-iare* that have a stressed *i*, for example *sciare, inviare*, have a double *i* in all the above forms, e.g. *scii*.

c) Verbs in *-ciare, -giare* and *-sciare*

Examples of verbs in this category are *cominciare, viaggiare* and *lasciare*. These verbs also have just one *i* in the forms mentioned in b), but drop the *i* of the stem in the future and conditional:

comincerò	comincerei
viaggerò	viaggerei
lascerò	lascerei

Irregular verbs

In the following table, only the verb parts which are formed irregularly are given. All other parts may be assumed to be regular.

For the future and conditional, only the first person singular is given in the table. For other persons, follow the regular pattern of endings:

Future: -ò, -ai, -à, -emo, -ete, -anno

Conditional: -ei, -esti, -ebbe, -emmo, -este, -ebbero

The *tu, noi* and *voi* forms of the imperative are identical to those forms of the present indicative, unless otherwise stated. The *Lei* and *Loro* forms are the third person singular and plural respectively of the present subjunctive.

	Present indicative	Present subjunctive	Present participle	Gerund	Imperative	Future	Conditional	Imperfect	Perfect	Past definite
andare to go	vado vai va andiamo andate vanno	vada vada vada andiamo andiate vadano			va' (vai) vada andiamo andate vadano	andrò	andrei		sono andato	
aprire to open									ho aperto	
avere to have	ho hai ha abbiamo avete hanno	abbia abbia abbia abbiamo abbiate abbiano			abbi abbia abbiamo abbiate abbiano	avrò	avrei			ebbi avesti ebbe avemmo aveste ebbero
bere to drink	bevo bevi beve beviamo bevete bevono	beva beva beva beviamo beviate bevano	bevente	bevendo		berrò	berrei	bevevo	ho bevuto	bevvi bevesti bevve bevemmo beveste bevvero

	Present	Present subjunctive	Present participle	Gerund	Imperative	Future	Conditional	Imperfect	Perfect	Past historic
cogliere to gather, pick	colgo cogli coglie cogliamo cogliete colgono	colga colga colga cogliamo cogliate colgano							ho colto	colsi cogliesti colse cogliemmo coglieste colsero
dare to give	do dai dà diamo date danno	dia dia dia diamo diate diano			da' (dai) dia diamo date diano	darò	darei			diedi (detti) desti diede (dette) demmo deste diedero (dettero)
dire to say	dico dici dice diciamo dite dicono	dica dica dica diciamo diciate dicano	dicente	dicendo	di' dica diciamo dite dicano			dicevo	ho detto	dissi dicesti disse dicemmo diceste dissero
dovere to have to	devo (debbo) devi deve dobbiamo dovete devono (debbono)	debba (deva) debba (deva) debba (deva) dobbiamo dobbiate debbano (devano)				dovrò	dovrei			

	Present indicative	Present subjunctive	Present participle	Gerund	Imperative	Future	Conditional	Imperfect	Perfect	Past definite
essere to be	sono sei è siamo siete sono	sia sia sia siamo siate siano			 sii sia siamo siate siano	sarò	sarei	ero eri era eravamo eravate erano	sono stato	fui fosti fu fummo foste furono
fare to do	faccio fai fa facciamo fate fanno	faccia faccia faccia facciamo facciate facciano	facente	facendo	 fa' (fai) faccia facciamo fate facciano	farò	farei	facevo	ho fatto	feci facesti fece facemmo faceste fecero
morire to die	muoio muori muore moriamo morite muoiono	muoia muoia muoia moriamo moriate muoiano				morirò (morrò)	morirei (morrei)		è morto	
piacere to please	piaccio piaci piace piacciamo piacete piacciono	piaccia piaccia piaccia piacciamo piacciate piacciano							sono piaciuto	piacqui piacesti piacque piacemmo piaceste piacquero

Verb	Present	Subjunctive	Participle	Gerund	Future	Conditional	Imperfect	Perfect	Past historic
porre to put	pongo poni pone poniamo ponete pongono	ponga ponga ponga poniamo poniate pongano	ponente	ponendo	porrò	porrei	ponevo	ho posto	posi ponesti pose ponemmo poneste posero
potere to be able	posso puoi può possiamo potete possono	possa possa possa possiamo possiate possano			potrò	potrei			
rimanere to stay	rimango rimani rimane rimaniamo rimanete rimangono	rimanga rimanga rimanga rimaniamo rimaniate rimangano			rimarrò	rimarrei		sono rimasto	rimasi rimanesti rimase rimanemmo rimaneste rimasero
salire to go up	salgo sali sale saliamo salite salgono	salga salga salga saliamo saliate salgano						sono salito, ho salito*	

	Present indicative	Present subjunctive	Present participle	Gerund	Imperative	Future	Conditional	Imperfect	Perfect	Past definite
sapere to know	so sai sa sappiamo sapete sanno	sappia sappia sappia sappiamo sappiate sappiano	sapiente		sappi sappia sappiamo sappiate sappiano	saprò	saprei			seppi sapesti seppe sapemmo sapeste seppero
scegliere to choose, prefer	scelgo scegli sceglie scegliamo scegliete scelgono	scelga scelga scelga scegliamo scegliate scelgano							ho scelto	scelsi scegliesti scelse scegliemmo sceglieste scelsero
sedere **(sedersi)** to sit	siedo siedi siede sediamo sedete siedono	sieda sieda sieda sediamo sediate siedano								
stare to stand, be	sto stai sta stiamo state stanno	stia stia stia stiamo stiate stiano			sta' (stai) stia stiamo state stiano	starò	starei		sono stato	stetti stesti stette stemmo steste stettero

	Present	Subjunctive	Future	Conditional	Perfect	Past historic
tenere to hold	tengo	tenga	terrò	terrei		tenni
	tieni	tenga				tenesti
	tiene	tenga				tenne
	teniamo	teniamo				tenemmo
	tenete	teniate				teneste
	tengono	tengano				tennero
uscire to go out	esco	esca			sono uscito	
	esci	esca				
	esce	esca				
	usciamo	usciamo				
	uscite	usciate				
	escono	escano				
venire to come	vengo	venga	verrò	verrei	sono venuto	venni
	vieni	venga				venisti
	viene	venga				venne
	veniamo	veniamo				venimmo
	venite	veniate				veniste
	vengono	vengano				vennero
volere to want	voglio	voglia	vorrò	vorrei		volli
	vuoi	voglia				volesti
	vuole	voglia				volle
	vogliamo	vogliamo				volemmo
	volete	vogliate				voleste
	vogliono	vogliano				vollero

*Verbs marked with an * by the perfect tense take the auxiliary *avere* when used transitively and *essere* when used intransitively (see pp. 64–65).

ANSWERS

1.1

I a, c, d, i

II b, c, f, h, i

1.1.1

III **a** parlare, to speak
b preparare, to prepare
c organizzare, to organise
d entrare, to enter **e** viaggiare, to travel **f** portare, to carry/take/wear **g** controllare, to check
h invitare, to invite **i** lavare, to wash **j** studiare, to study

IV **a** cucinare, to cook **b** cenare, to dine **c** spruzzare, to sprinkle
d congelare, to freeze **e** sgelare, to thaw **f** brasare, to braise
g versare, to pour **h** tagliare, to cut
i mangiare, to eat **j** pranzare, to lunch **k** mescolare, to mix

V **a** to begin, cominciare **b** to accept, accettare **c** to separate, separare **d** to evaluate, valutare
e to steal, rubare **f** to sail, navigare
g to publish, pubblicare **h** to turn, girare **i** to continue, continuare
j to end, terminare

1.1.2

VI **a** 2 vend **b** 1 mostr **c** 1 cant
d 3 sal **e** 1 lav **f** 2 conclud
g 1 ascolt **h** 2 chiud **i** 1 lasci
j 2 prend **k** 2 scegli **l** 1 port
m 1 torn **n** 3 ven **o** 3 dorm

1.1.3

VII **a** to know how to, sapere
b to see, vedere **c** to have, avere
d to go, andare **e** to be able to, potere **f** to have to, dovere **g** to want to, volere **h** to take, prendere
i to be, essere **j** to do, fare

1.1.4

VIII **a** io **b** lei **c** lui **d** noi
e voi **f** Lei **g** loro **h** loro

IX **a** lui **b** lei **c** lui **d** loro
e loro **f** noi **g** io **h** loro **i** loro
j noi

1.2

I **a** scaricare **b** telefonare
c accompagnare **d** andare
e portare **f** prendere **g** volare
h visitare **i** studiare **j** cenare

1.2.1

II **a** I am singing **b** you are eating (familiar sing.) **c** he/she/it is drinking, you (formal sing.) are drinking **d** we are working **e** you are travelling (familiar pl.)
f they/you (formal pl.) are going up

III **a** sto lavorando **b** stai sognando **c** stiamo guardando
d sta leggendo **e** sta bevendo
f stanno mangiando **g** state viaggiando **h** stanno partendo

1.2.2

IV **a** parlo **b** studio **c** porto **d** lavoro **e** ascolto **f** suono **g** visito **h** guardo **i** arrivo **j** spiego

V **a** Lavoro **b** Arrivo **c** Parcheggio **d** Entro **e** Saluto **f** Uso **g** Cerco **h** Entro **i** Cerco **j** Lavoro

VI **a** entro **b** compro **c** chiamo **d** provo **e** pago **f** mando **g** spero **h** cerco **i** butto **j** amo

VII **a** parlo **b** viaggio **c** passo **d** chiamo **e** arrivo **f** entro **g** compro **h** aspetto **i** ceno **j** mando **k** chiacchiero **l** invito **m** telefono **n** guardo

VIII **a** prendere **b** chiedere **c** correre **d** rispondere **e** vendere **f** leggere **g** bere **h** vedere **i** mettere **j** credere

IX **a** bevo **b** prendo **c** corro **d** leggo **e** vendo **f** chiedo **g** metto **h** credo **i** vedo **j** rispondo

X **a** dormo **b** seguo **c** parto **d** sento **e** offro **f** capisco **g** preferisco **h** spedisco

XI **a** apro **b** suggerisco **c** garantisco **d** copro **e** soffro **f** costruisco **g** scopro **h** contribuisco **i** pulisco

XII **a** scopro **b** pulisco **c** apro **d** garantisco **e** copro **f** suggerisco

XIII **a** tengo **b** salgo **c** conosco **d** tengo **e** rimango **f** conosco **g** vengo **h** risalgo **i** ritengo

XIV **a** voglio **b** ho **c** do **d** devo **e** posso **f** so **g** sono **h** vado

XV **a** mi sveglio **b** mi alzo **c** mi faccio la barba **d** mi lavo **e** mi pettino **f** mi vesto **g** mi siedo **h** mi annoio **i** mi arrabbio **j** mi addormento

XVI **a** mi fa male **b** mi rimangono **c** mi rimane **d** mi piace **e** mi interessa **f** mi piacciono **g** mi interessano **h** mi fanno male

1.2.3

XVII **a** compri **b** bevi **c** vivi **d** parli **e** guardi **f** vendi **g** ascolti **h** scrivi **i** lavi **j** lavori

XVIII **a** vieni **b** studi **c** mangi **d** cerchi **e** paghi **f** tieni **g** vieni **h** siedi

XIX **a** sei **b** hai **c** vai **d** vuoi **e** puoi **f** stai **g** sai **h** esci **i** dici **j** devi

XX **a** ii **b** iv **c** v **d** iii **e** i

XXI **a** ti fanno male **b** ti rimane **c** ti rimangono **d** ti piace **e** ti va di **f** ti piacciono **g** ti interessano

XXII **a** hai **b** parti **c** prendi **d** arrivi **e** ceni **f** torni

XXIII **a** iii **b** vi **c** v **d** vii **e** i **f** ix **g** iv **h** ii **i** x **j** viii

1.2.4

XXIV **a** scrive **b** canta **c** naviga **d** legge **e** riceve **f** vende **g** desidera **h** presta **i** prepara **j** firma

XXV **a** va **b** dice **c** può **d** sa **e** vuole **f** vuole **g** esce **h** deve **i** siede **j** muore

XXVI **a** è **b** vuole **c** deve **d** va **e** sa **f** arriva **g** ha **h** mette **i** chiama **j** torna

XXVII **a** si sveglia **b** si alza **c** si fa la barba **d** si lava **e** si asciuga **f** si pettina **g** si veste **h** si lava **i** si siede **j** si annoia **k** si mette **l** si stanca **m** si riposa

XXVIII suggested answers: **a** vuole/desidera **b** fuma **c** mangia **d** beve **e** preferisce

XXIX **a** ha **b** parte **c** prende **d** arriva **e** cena **f** torna

XXX **a** legge **b** va **c** prende **d** dorme **e** fa **f** prende **g** deve **h** dice

1.2.5

XXXI **a** lavoriamo **b** giochiamo **c** vediamo **d** ceniamo **e** torniamo **f** andiamo **g** partiamo **h** arriviamo **i** compriamo **j** abbiamo

XXXII **a** siamo **b** parliamo **c** andiamo **d** scegliamo **e** prendiamo **f** cambiamo **g** capiamo **h** alloggiamo/stiamo **i** mangiamo **j** facciamo **k** finiamo **l** giochiamo

XXXIII **a** ci svegliamo **b** ci alziamo **c** ci laviamo **d** ci riposiamo **e** ci vestiamo **f** ci sediamo **g** ci addormentiamo **h** ci separiamo

XXXIV **a** we have, abbiamo **b** we are, siamo **c** we are staying, rimaniamo **d** we are eating, mangiamo **e** we can, possiamo **f** we are not coming, non veniamo **g** we do not understand, non capiamo **h** we want, vogliamo **i** we are going, andiamo **j** we are seeing, vediamo **k** we are leaving, partiamo **l** we are arriving, arriviamo **m** we are coming, veniamo **n** we are doing, facciamo **o** we are reading, leggiamo

1.2.6

XXXVI **a** Can you remember this man? Vi ricordate di questo signore? **b** Are you having a rest? Vi riposate? **c** Are you getting dressed already? Vi vestite già? **d** Are you having fun? Vi divertite? **e** Do you get up late? Vi alzate tardi? **f** Do you wake up early? Vi svegliate presto?

1.2.7

XXXVII **a** vogliono **b** hanno **c** vanno **d** lasciano **e** fanno **f** escono **g** riescono **h** cercano **i** vedono **j** devono

XXXVIII **a** si riposano **b** si svegliano **c** si alzano **d** si lavano **e** si preparano **f** escono **g** vanno **h** arrivano **i** si annoiano **j** se ne vanno

1.2.8

XXXIX **a** ho **b** sono **c** vado **d** prendo **e** scendo **f** esco **g** attraverso **h** aspetto **i** voglio **j** torno

XL **a** hai **b** sei **c** vai **d** prendi **e** scendi **f** esci **g** attraversi **h** aspetti **i** vuoi **j** torni

XLI **a** ha **b** è **c** va **d** prende **e** scende **f** esce **g** attraversa **h** aspetta **i** vuole **j** torna

XLII **a** abbiamo **b** siamo **c** andiamo **d** prendiamo **e** scendiamo **f** usciamo **g** attraversiamo **h** aspettiamo **i** vogliamo **j** torniamo

XLIII **a** avete **b** siete **c** andate **d** prendete **e** scendete **f** uscite **g** attraversate **h** aspettate **i** volete **j** tornate

XLIV   a hanno   **b** sono   **c** vanno
d prendono   **e** scendono
f escono   **g** attraversano
h aspettano   **i** vogliono   **j** tornano

1.3.1

I   a non bevono   **b** non scrivo
c non legge   **d** non compriamo
e non so   **f** non riesce   **g** non
vengono   **h** non voglio   **i** non ci
piace   **j** non mangi

1.3.2

II
a Abitano a Brescia i signori
Bianchi?
b Vanno in vacanza loro?
c Prendono il treno loro?
d Vanno alla Costa Amalfitana
loro?
e Hanno un appartamento lì loro?
f Affittano una macchina loro?
g Giocano a golf loro?
h Praticano lo sci acquatico loro?
i Hanno degli amici Positano loro?
j La sera cenano in un ristorante
loro?

III
a Dove vanno loro?
b Quando partono loro?
c Come viaggiano loro?
d Perché stanno a Bari loro?
e Che fanno loro?
f Con chi hanno una riunione
loro?
g Quanto tempo stanno in albergo
loro?

1.3.3

IV   a Come on! Dai!   **b** Go! Va!
c Do sit down! Si accomodi!
d Turn left! Giri a sinistra!
e Listen! Ascoltate!   **f** Wait!
Aspetta!   **g** Hold the line!
(telephone) Resti in linea!

h Hurry up! Fai presto!

V   a sta'   **b** non ti sedere/sederti
c fai/fa'   **d** dammi   **e** fai/fa'
f non venire   **g** va'   **h** alzati

VI
a Enter your PIN. Inserire il
numero di codice segreto.
b Pull. Tirare.
c Wait for the tone. Aspetti il
segnale di libero.
d Speak into the microphone. Parli
vicino al microfono.
e Sign here. Firmi qui.
f Cancel your ticket. Timbri il suo
biglietto.
g Push. Spingere.
h Please hold the line. Per favore,
rimanga in linea.
i Wait. Aspetti.
j Press the button. Prema il
pulsante.
k Listen, please. Senta, per favore.
l Hello. (= tell me – e.g. answering
phone) Dica.

VII   a sieda   **b** vada   **c** beva
d mangi   **e** venga   **f** fumi
g faccia   **h** prenda   **i** vada
j dorma

VIII   parlare; to sell; partano;
finire; look for ...!; to pay; vadano;
to drink; dia; say/tell!; to be; fare; to
remain/stay; salga; sappiano; stare;
esca; to come

IX   a usciamo   **b** rimaniamo a
casa   **c** guardiamo la TV
d mangiamo   **e** alziamoci

X   a gira/giri   **b** sali/salga
c prendi/prenda   **d** va'/vada
e continua/continui
f guarda/guardi   **g** attraversa/
atraversi   **h** prendi/prenda
i scendi/scenda   **j** mandami/
mi mandi

XI **a** passi **b** mangi **c** beva
d faccia **e** chiuda **f** apra
g faccia vedere **h** parli **i** venga

XII **a** entrate **b** mettetevi
c trovate **d** correte **e** state
f allungate **g** fate **h** abbassate
i flettete **j** vi muovete/muovetevi

XIII **a** escano **b** girino
c prendano **d** vadano
e attraversino **f** seguano **g** girino

XIV

a Don't open the door. (tu) Non
aprire la porta.
b Don't walk on the grass. (voi)
Non calpestate l'erba.
c Don't eat in the shop. (voi) Non
mangiate nel negozio.
d Don't drink the water. (Lei) Non
beva l'acqua.
e Don't cross the road here. (voi)
Non attraversate la strada qui.
f Don't lean out of the window.
(Loro) Non si sporgetevi dal
finestrino.
g Don't leave your luggage here.
(tu) Non lasciare i bagagli qui.
h Don't wait here. (voi) Non
aspettate qui.
i Don't put your boots on the table.
(Lei) Non metta gli stivali sul
tavolo.
j Don't wear black. (tu) Non vestirti
di nero.
k Don't smoke. (Loro) Non fumino.

XV **a** prepara **b** taglia **c** friggi
d batti **e** aggiungi **f** metti
g mescola **h** riscalda **i** versa
j friggi **k** gira **l** friggi

1.4

I **a** perfect **b** perfect **c** perfect
d imperfect **e** perfect
f imperfect **g** imperfect
h imperfect **i** perfect **j** imperfect

1.4.1

II **a** ho **b** hai parlato **c** ha
parlato **d** hanno parlato **e** hanno
f abbiamo venduto **g** avete
venduto **h** ha **i** ha capito
j abbiamo capito

III **a** abbiamo **b** hanno **c** ha
d ha **e** avete **f** hanno **g** hai
h ho **i** ha **j** ha

IV **a** andato **b** tornata
c arrivata **d** usciti **e** alzati
f venute

V **a** è arrivato **b** si è svegliata
c siamo partiti **d** si sono divertiti
e sono andati **f** è venuta

1.4.2

VI **a** giocato **b** mangiato
c finito **d** venduto **e** ascoltato
f ripetuto **g** tenuto **h** aspettato
i sistemato **j** invitato **k** lavato
l rivenduto **m** fermato **n** potuto
o tirato **p** dimenticato **q** uscito
r entrato **s** sentito **t** partito

VII **a** giocato **b** invitato
c chiamato **d** parlato **e** assicurato
f studiato **g** mandato **h** cambiato
i stampata **j** stampati **k** mandate
l guardato

VIII **a** visto **b** scritto **c** immesso
d fatto **e** detto **f** chiesto

IX **a** ha vinto **b** ha voluto **c** ha
visto **d** ha comprato **e** è piaciuta
f ha deciso **g** ha messo **h** ha
preso **i** ha visto **j** ha creduto
k ha seguito **l** è andato **m** ha
fermato **n** ha dovuto

X

a Sofia ha letto il suo ultimo
romanzo.
b Hai/Ha/Avete letto il libro?

c Non abbiamo letto il libro.
d Hanno visto il film del libro.
e Sofia ha visto il film ieri.
f Non abbiamo ancora visto il film.
g Hai/Ha/Avete/Hanno visto il film?

1.4.3

XI **a** mi sono alzato **b** si è alzato
c si è alzata **d** si è alzato **e** si sono
alzati **f** si è alzata **g** ci siamo
alzati **h** si sono alzati **i** vi siete
alzate **j** ti sei alzato

1.4.5

XII **a** dormiva **b** guardava
c leggeva **d** chiacchieravo
e parlavamo **f** faceva **g** telefonava
h riparavano **i** giocavano

XIII **a** era **b** facevano **c** eravamo
d eri **e** bevevo **f** dicevi

XIV **a** aspettavo **b** ascoltavi
c andavamo **d** leggeva
e aspettava **f** usciva **g** stavano
h faceva **i** guardavate **j** beveva

XV **a** faceva **b** nevicava **c** era
d tirava **e** pioveva **f** tuonava
g si dissolveva **h** faceva **i** era
j era

XVI **a** era, abitava **b** erano
c era/erano **d** coltivava
e lavoravano **f** raccoglievano
g facevano **h** era **i** cucinava
j doveva **k** voleva

1.4.6

XVII **a** abitavano/è nata **b** era/è
andata **c** aveva/è nato **d** ha
avuto/aveva **e** attraversava/si è
fermata **f** ha visto/aspettava
g aveva/ha dato **h** studiava/ha
deciso **i** faceva/ha visto
j lavorava/ha conosciuto **k** era/ha
fatto **l** faceva/si sono sposati

1.4.7

XVIII **1** andammo **2** stemmo
3 affittammo **4** fece **5** passai
6 vennero **7** divertimmo
8 cenammo **9** ballammo
10 facemmo **11** andaste **12** faceste

1.5.1

I **a** guarderemo **b** preparerai
c metterete **d** mangeranno
e permetterà **f** scriverà
g arriveranno **h** entreremo
i partirò **j** saliranno

II **a** porterò **b** porterà
c porterà **d** porterà
e porteranno **f** porteranno
g porteremo **h** porterà **i** porterai

III **a** avrò **b** verrete **c** farai
d avremo **e** salirà **f** saprà
g vorranno **h** diremo **i** metterete
j potranno **k** terrà **l** verrò

IV **a** avrò **b** andrò **c** farò
d manderò **e** verrai **f** andremo
g potremo/sarà/costerà
h finirò/tornerò/lavorerò

V **a** andrò **b** andrai **c** andrà
d andrà **e** andremo **f** andrete
g andranno **h** andranno
i andranno **j** andrò

VI **a** -anno **b** -à **c** -à **d** -anno
e -à **f** -à **g** -à **h** -emo **i** -à
j -ete

VII **a** partiremo **b** prenderete
c aspetterà/porterà **d** potrete
e pranzerete/vorrete **f** potrete
g farà/dovrete

1.5.3

VIII **a** mangerei **b** berrei
c dormirei **d** parlerei **e** vivrei
f comprerei **g** chiederei
h ascolterei **i** guarderei

IX **a** giocherei **b** giocherebbe
c giocherebbero **d** giocheremmo
e giochereste

X **a** preferirei **b** preferirebbe
c preferirebbero **d** preferiremmo
e preferireste

XI **a** mi piacerebbe **b** piacerebbe
c interesserebbe **d** interesserebbe
e ti piacerebbero **f** vi piacerebbe
g Le piacerebbe
h interesserebbero

XII **a** preparerei **b** uscirei
c avrei **d** direi **e** verrei **f** potrei
g metterei **h** saprei **i** vorrei
j avrei

XIII **a** potrebbe **b** potremmo
c potremmo **d** potrei **e** potresti
f potrebbe **g** potrebbero
h potremmo **i** potremmo
j potremmo

1.6.3

I **a** venire **b** prendere **c** fare
d sentirsi **e** essere **f** avere
g sapere **h** potere **i** avere
j volere

1.9.1

I **a** essere **b** essere **c** essere
d stare **e** essere

1.9.3

III **a** abbiamo ragione **b** non hai
ragione **c** ho caldo **d** ha sete
e hanno fame **f** abbiamo freddo
g ho sete **h** ha molto sonno
i abbiamo fortuna **j** ho fretta
k non hanno ragione **l** ho molto
freddo **m** hanno caldo
n abbiamo sete **o** ho paura dei
ragni **p** hai sete? **q** ha freddo?
r avete caldo? **s** hanno fame?
t hai ragione? **u** non ha ragione
v avete paura? **w** non ho paura

x non ha paura **y** non abbiamo
paura **z** ha sempre ragione

IV **a** Ho mal di testa/la testa mi fa
male **b** Hai mal di denti/ti fanno
male i denti? **c** Ha mal di piedi/le
fa male il piede **d** Mi fanno male
le braccia **e** Gli fa male il
ginocchio **f** Ha mal di testa/le fa
male la testa? **g** Lei ha mal
d'orecchio/le fa male l'orecchio
h Vi fanno male gli occhi?
i Hanno mal di schiena/gli fa male
la schiena? **j** Ha mal di schiena/la
schiena gli fa male

1.9.4

V **a** conosco **b** conosce **c** sanno
d conosciamo **e** ha conosciuto
f conoscevano **g** conosceva
h sappiamo **i** sanno **j** sa **k** so

1.9.5

VI **a** piove molto nel Regno Unito
b fa caldo in Italia **c** è
mezzogiorno **d** sono le nove e un
quarto **e** bisogna riposare!
f manca pane **g** si tratta del
motore **h** ci vuole un giorno per
andare in Italia

1.9.8

VII **a** Ricordo John **b** Lui si
ricorda di me **c** Si ricorda della.
mia casa **d** Ricordiamo le nostre
vacanze **e** Mi sono dimenticato di
mia moglie **f** Non mi ricordo del
suo sorriso **g** I miei figli non
hanno dimenticato la loro madre

1.9.9

VIII **a** Io non sono mai stato in
Italia. **b** Loro non hanno fatto
male a nessuno. **c** Non vedo mai
Anna. **d** Non hanno niente nella
loro casa. **e** Non hai mai imparato

a nuotare? **f** Io non vedo nessuno.
g Lei non va mai in bicicletta.
h Non ho niente in tasca.   **i** Non sono mai stato a Massa Carrara.
j Nessuno è a casa.

IX
a We haven't anyting to eat. Non abbiamo niente da mangiare.
b Nobody has been shopping. Nessuno ha fatto la spesa.
c I didn't have time to go to town. Non ho avuto tempo per andare in città.
d There is no bread or cheese. Non c'è né pane né formaggio.
e You never go to the supermarket. Non vai mai al supermercato.
f I haven't any money. Non ho soldi.

1.9.10
X   **a** dove   **b** come   **c** quando
d perché   **e** che   **f** quando
g quanti   **h** chi

1.9.11
XI
a Abito qui da …
giorni/settimane/mesi/anni
b Imparo l'italiano da …
c Conosco il/la mio/mia migliore amico/amica da …

XII
a Pino has just got home.
b My friend has just rung me.
c We have just eaten dinner.
d My parents have just sold their house.
e I have just finished my work.

2
I   sister, restaurant, market, morning, vegetables, soup, lunch, dishes, night, fridge

2.2.1
I   **a** la   **b** l'   **c** il   **d** la   **e** la   **f** lo   **g** l'   **h** l'   **i** la   **j** lo   **k** il

II   **a** la   **b** la   **c** la   **d** la   **e** il   **f** il   **g** la   **h** il   **i** l'   **j** il

III   **a** l'   **b** il   **c** la   **d** il   **e** l'   **f** l'   **g** il   **h** la   **i** lo   **j** la   **k** il   **l** il   **m** l'   **n** il   **o** l'   **p** la   **q** la   **r** la   **s** la   **t** il

2.3
I   **a** i cani   **b** i gatti   **c** le barche   **d** le terrazze   **e** le macchine   **f** le moto   **g** i castelli   **h** i tedeschi   **i** i pacchi

2.4
I   **a** un   **b** una   **c** un   **d** una   **e** uno   **f** una   **g** un   **h** una   **i** una   **j** un

II   **a** Vittorio è medico   **b** Chiara è studentessa   **c** Ermenegildo è insegnante   **d** Toni è americano   **e** Enrico è cattolico   **f** È disoccupato   **g** È autista

III   **a** un   **b** un   **c** una   **d** un   **e** delle, dei   **f** un, dei, delle, degli   **g** dei, dei, un   **h** un

2.5
I   **a** l'   **b** la   **c** il   **d** l'   **e** la   **f** l'   **g** la   **h** lo   **i** lo   **j** lo   **k** la   **l** la   **m** l'   **n** la   **o** il   **p** la   **q** il   **r** la   **s** la   **t** il

2.6.1
I   **a** il mio   **b** la mia   **c** la mia   **d** il mio   **e** il mio   **f** la mia   **g** la mia   **h** la mia   **i** il mio   **j** la mia

II   **a** i miei   **b** le mie   **c** i miei   **d** le mie   **e** i miei   **f** le mie   **g** le mie   **h** i miei   **i** i miei   **j** i miei

III **a** i miei **b** mio **c** mia **d** mio **e** mia **f** mia **g** i miei **h** (la) mia **i** (il) mio **j** le mie **k** mio

2.6.2

IV **a** i tuoi **b** tuo **c** tua **d** le tue **e** tuo **f** i tuoi **g** tuo **h** le tue **i** il tuo **j** i tuoi

V **a** le tue **b** il tuo/la tua **c** il tuo **d** le tue **e** i tuoi **f** la tua **g** tuo **h** le tue **i** i tuoi **j** tua

2.6.3

VI **a** le sue **b** suo **c** suo **d** sua **e** suo **f** le sue **g** il suo **h** il suo **i** i suoi **j** il suo

VII **a** La sua **b** (Il) suo **c** I suoi **d** Sua **e** i suoi **f** Il suo **g** Il suo **h** I suoi **i** Il suo **j** Le sue

2.6.4

VIII **a** la nostra **b** il nostro **c** i nostri **d** il nostro **e** i nostri **f** il nostro **g** la nostra **h** il nostro **i** il nostro **j** le nostre

2.6.5

IX **a** la vostra **b** la vostra **c** le vostre **d** i vostri **e** i vostri **f** i vostri **g** il vostro **h** la vostra **i** la vostra **j** le vostre

2.6.6

X **a** la loro **b** il loro **c** le loro **d** il loro **e** i loro **f** le loro **g** la loro **h** la loro **i** le loro **j** il loro

2.6.7

XI **a** il suo **b** la sua **c** i suoi **d** i suoi **e** la sua **f** le sue **g** i suoi **h** la sua **i** la sua **j** la sua

2.7.1

I **a** quel **b** questa **c** questo **d** queste **e** quei **f** quest' **g** quella **h** queste **i** quel **j** questa

2.7.2

II **a** Quante **b** Quanti **c** Quanti **d** Quanto **e** Quanto (latte is masculine singular!)

3.1.8

I **a** io **b** noi **c** loro **d** essa **e** lui **f** lei **g** tu/Lei/voi/Loro

II **a** lui **b** loro **c** noi **d** tu **e** lei **f** io **g** lei **h** voi **i** noi **j** voi

3.2

I **a** new car **b** it **c** a cat **d** a tree **e** the wing mirror **f** a bunch of flowers **g** the car

3.2.1

II **a** La **b** Lo **c** Le/Li **d** l' **e** L' **f** Lo

3.3

I **a** me **b** her **c** me **d** him **e** me **f** her **g** me **h** him **i** her **j** him **k** me **l** me

3.3.1

II **a** mi **b** ci **c** loro **d** le **e** vi **f** ti **g** ti **h** le **i** gli **j** ci

3.3.3

III **a** Me l'ha dato **b** Gliel'ho scritto **c** Gliel'ha dato **d** Te l'hanno dato **e** Ce l'hai dato **f** Gliel'ha comprato **g** Me l'ha letto **h** Ce l'ha dato **i** Ve l'abbiamo dato **j** Gliel'hanno letto **k** Me l'ha dato **l** Non te lo darò

3.4

I a lui **b** lei **c** loro **d** lei
e lui, lei **f** noi **g** lei **h** loro
i voi **j** lei

3.4.1

II a Guardaci! **b** Dammelo!
c Fallo! **d** Svegliati! **e** Scrivilo!

3.5

I a Quanta **b** Quante **c** Quale
d (Che) cosa **e** Di chi **f** Quanto
g (Che) cosa **h** Quanti **i** Quale
j Chi

3.6

I a il mio **b** mia **c** il mio **d** la
mia **e** mie **f** i miei **g** le mie
h miei

3.7.4

I a che **b** che **c** con chi **d** la
cui **e** di cui **f** che

4.1.2

III

3.8

I a questo **b** questi **c** queste
d questa **e** questo **f** questa
g questo **h** queste **i** queste
j questi

II a quella **b** quelli **c** quella
d quelli **e** quelle **f** quello
g quelle **h** quello **i** quella
j quelli

4.1

I a short, fat **b** long, blonde,
green **c** new **d** new, casual
e large, old **f** tall, dark **g** small
h older, younger **i** favourite **j** cold

4.1.1

II a nuovo/vecchio **b** nuova/
vecchia **c** nuovi/vecchi
d nuove/vecchie **e** nuovo/vecchio
f nuova/vecchia **g** nuovi/vecchi
h nuove/vecchie

		Singular		Plural	
		Masc.	**Fem.**	**Masc.**	**Fem.**
a	happy	contento	contenta	contenti	contente
b	beautiful	bello	bella	belli	belle
c	ugly	brutto	brutta	brutti	brutte
d	tall	alto	alta	alti	alte
e	short	basso	bassa	bassi	basse
f	good	buono	buona	buoni	buone
g	bad	cattivo	cattiva	cattivi	cattive
h	quiet	tranquillo	tranquilla	tranquilli	tranquille
i	noisy	rumoroso	rumorosa	rumorosi	rumorose
j	strange	strano	strana	strani	strane
k	shy	timido	timida	timidi	timide
l	serious	serio	seria	seri	serie
m	frivolous	{poco serio {frivolo	poco seria frivola	poco seri frivoli	poco serie frivole
n	sensible	sensato	sensata	sensati	sensate
o	stupid	stupido	stupida	stupidi	stupide

	Singular		Plural	
	Masc.	**Fem.**	**Masc.**	**Fem.**
p sincere	sincero	sincera	sinceri	sincere
q insincere	insincero	insincera	insinceri	insincere
r thin	magro	magra	magri	magre
s fat	grasso	grassa	grassi	grasse
t short (thing)	corto	corta	corti	corte

4.1.3

IV **a** comunista **b** chiacchierona
c viola **d** lisce **e** pochi,
poveri/povere **f** blu **g** marrone
h lunghi **i** poca **j** belle **k** forti
l begli **m** pubblici **n** Gran
o grandi **p** Buon **q** grande
r chiacchieroni **s** forti **t** saggi

V **a** tedesco **b** inglese
c americana **d** italiano
e spagnoli **f** inglesi **g** svizzero
h americani **i** scozzese
j canadesi

4.1.4

VI **a** rossa **b** marrone **c** verde
d azzurro **e** arancione **f** bianche
g viola **h** gialli **i** nera **j** grigi
k rosa

4.4.1

I **a** più veloce **b** più bella **c** più
grandi **d** più interessanti **e** più
difficile **f** più bello **g** più cara
h più poveri **i** più cara **j** più bella

II **a** più **b** più **c** meno **d** più
e più **f** meno **g** meno **h** più
i meno **j** più

4.4.2

III **a** più **b** più **c** più **d** più
e meno **f** meno

4.4.3

IV **a** tanto grande quanto **b** più
grande della **c** meno grande del
d più grandi dei **e** più grande della

4.4.4

V **a** migliore **b** peggiori
c maggiore **d** minore **e** minori
f migliori

5.1.2

I **a** seccamente **b** follemente
c semplicemente **d** rapidamente
e facilmente **f** regolarmente
g raramente **h** male **i** veramente
j bene

6.2.6

I **a** in **b** in **c** in **d** in **e** al
f in **g** al **h** alla **i** in **j** al

II **a** al **b** alla **c** delle **d** del
e della **f** di **g** di **h** degli **i** di
j al

III **a** a, con **b** al **c** con **d** per
e con, a **f** in **g** con **h** sopra